UTAH

DRIVER'S LICENSE

HANDBOOK

2025

Your Complete Guide to Traffic Laws, Safe Driving Practices,
and Licensing Requirements with Updated Regulations and
Tips to ace your Exam with confidence

ALEX RYDER

Thank you for purchasing this handbook. We hope you find it useful and informative in your journey to obtaining your driver's permit. Best of luck on your exam and safe driving!

Thank you for purchasing this handbook. We hope you find it useful and informative in your journey to obtaining your driver's permit. Best of luck on your exam and safe driving!

TABLE OF CONTENTS

Introduction

Every year, millions of new drivers take to the roads across the United States, including here in Utah. Behind each of these drivers lies a journey that began with a critical milestone: passing the state's licensing process. Consider this—according to national statistics, traffic accidents are the leading cause of death for individuals aged 15 to 20. While sobering, this statistic underscores an important truth: driving is not just a privilege; it is a responsibility that can impact countless lives. Passing the Utah DMV exam is more than a step toward obtaining your license—it's a gateway to becoming a safe and conscientious driver, fully equipped to navigate the roads responsibly.

Imagine this scenario: a newly licensed driver faces their first winter storm on Utah's winding mountain roads. Without adequate preparation and knowledge, their reaction to icy conditions could mean the difference between a close call and a tragic accident. This handbook aims to ensure that every driver is equipped with the skills, knowledge, and mindset to handle such challenges confidently and safely.

By choosing to prepare for your driver's license through this comprehensive guide, you're taking the first step toward becoming a competent and informed driver. Passing the DMV exam is not just about memorizing facts or answering multiple-choice questions—it's about understanding traffic laws, mastering defensive driving techniques, and developing habits that ensure safety for yourself, your passengers, and others on the road.

This handbook is designed to be more than a study guide. It's a roadmap to success, both in passing your exam and in adopting safe driving practices that will last a lifetime. Within these pages, you'll find everything you need: clear explanations of Utah's traffic laws, detailed insights into road signs and regulations, tips for mastering defensive driving, and practical strategies for navigating Utah's unique driving conditions.

Safe driving saves lives, reduces stress, and empowers communities. By dedicating yourself to learning and applying the principles outlined in this handbook, you're not just preparing for a test— you're investing in a future of responsible and safe driving that benefits everyone who shares the road with you.

Welcome to your journey. Let's get started.

Chapter 1

Understanding the Licensing Process

The Utah Department of Motor Vehicles (DMV) plays a crucial role in ensuring the safety and efficiency of the state's transportation system. As the regulatory body responsible for issuing driver's licenses and vehicle registrations, the Utah DMV ensures that drivers are adequately prepared to operate vehicles on public roads. Its mission extends beyond licensing; the DMV aims to promote road safety, enforce compliance with traffic laws, and provide essential services to residents.

The Utah DMV offers a variety of services designed to meet the needs of drivers and vehicle owners. These services include issuing learner's permits, standard driver's licenses, commercial driver's licenses (CDLs), and identification cards. Additionally, the DMV oversees vehicle registration and titling, ensuring that vehicles meet safety and emissions standards. It also manages driver records, processes reinstatements of suspended or revoked licenses, and provides access to educational resources for drivers of all levels.

For new drivers, the DMV is the gateway to safe and legal driving. It administers the written knowledge test, road skills test, and vision test required for obtaining a license. Beyond licensing, the DMV enforces regulations related to insurance requirements and license renewals. Its role in maintaining accurate records helps law enforcement agencies and insurance companies verify compliance with state laws.

The Utah DMV's commitment to public safety extends to offering resources and guidance on topics such as defensive driving, traffic laws, and the consequences of impaired or distracted driving. Whether you are applying for your first license or renewing an existing one, the Utah DMV is a vital resource for navigating the licensing process and ensuring compliance with state regulations.

Types of Licenses in Utah

Utah offers several types of driver's licenses to accommodate the diverse needs of its residents. Each license type is tailored to specific purposes, and understanding these options is essential when deciding which one to apply for.

Learner's Permit

The learner's permit is designed for individuals who are beginning their driving journey. Applicants must be at least 15 years old and pass a written knowledge test and vision test. The permit allows individuals to practice driving under the supervision of a licensed adult aged 21 or older. It is valid for one year and is a prerequisite for obtaining a full driver's license.

Standard Driver's License

The standard driver's license is the most common license issued in Utah. It permits individuals to operate non-commercial vehicles. Applicants must complete a driver education course, pass the written and road skills tests, and meet the age requirement of 16 years. Those under 18 must hold a learner's permit for at least six months before applying.

Commercial Driver's License (CDL)

A CDL is required for individuals who wish to operate commercial vehicles such as trucks and buses. Applicants must meet federal and state requirements, including passing specialized knowledge and skills tests. CDLs are categorized into Class A, B, and C licenses, depending on the type of vehicle operated.

Motorcycle Endorsement

Individuals who wish to operate motorcycles must obtain a motorcycle endorsement. This requires passing a written test and a motorcycle skills test. Applicants must already hold a standard driver's license or learner's permit.

Identification Cards

For residents who do not wish to drive but need official identification, the Utah DMV issues state ID cards. These cards are often used for voting, travel, and other identification purposes.

Each license type has specific eligibility requirements, so it is essential to understand these criteria before applying. Choosing the appropriate license ensures you can legally and safely operate your chosen vehicle.

Steps to Obtaining Your License

Obtaining a driver's license in Utah is a multi-step process designed to ensure applicants are prepared to drive safely. Below is a step-by-step guide to help you navigate the process:

1. **Determine Eligibility**: Ensure you meet the age and residency requirements. Applicants must be at least 15 years

old for a learner's permit and 16 years old for a standard driver's license.

2. **Prepare Required Documents**: Gather the necessary identification documents, proof of residency, and Social Security number (see "Required Documents and Eligibility" for details).

3. **Complete a Driver Education Course**: For applicants under 19, completing a state-approved driver education course is mandatory. This includes classroom instruction and behind-the-wheel training.

4. **Obtain a Learner's Permit**: Pass the written knowledge test and vision test to receive a learner's permit. This allows you to practice driving under supervision.

5. **Practice Driving**: Accumulate the required number of supervised driving hours. Drivers under 18 must complete at least 40 hours of practice, including 10 hours at night.

6. **Schedule and Take the Road Test**: Once you feel confident in your driving skills, schedule a road test at a DMV office. During the test, you will demonstrate your ability to operate a vehicle safely.

7. **Pass the Vision Test**: A vision test is required to ensure you can see well enough to drive safely.

8. **Pay Fees and Receive Your License**: After passing all tests, pay the applicable fees, and your license will be issued. Drivers under 18 will receive a provisional license with restrictions, such as limits on night-time driving and passenger numbers.

Following these steps ensures a smooth path to obtaining your license. Proper preparation is key to passing the required tests and becoming a safe and responsible driver.

Required Documents and Eligibility

The application process for a driver's license in Utah requires specific documentation to verify your identity, residency, and eligibility. Ensuring you have the necessary documents in advance will save time and prevent delays.

Required Documents

1. **Proof of Identity**: Acceptable documents include a valid passport, birth certificate, or permanent resident card.

2. **Social Security Number (SSN)**: Provide your SSN card or a W-2 form displaying your number.

3. **Proof of Utah Residency**: Submit two documents that show your current Utah address, such as utility bills, rental agreements, or bank statements.

4. **Parental Consent (for Minors)**: Applicants under 18 must have a parent or legal guardian sign a consent form.

5. **Driver Education Completion Certificate**: If required, provide proof of completing a state-approved driver education course.

Eligibility Criteria

1. **Age Requirements**: Applicants must be at least 15 years old for a learner's permit and 16 years old for a standard license.

2. **Residency**: You must be a legal resident of Utah. Temporary residents, such as students, may have additional requirements.

3. **Physical and Mental Fitness**: Applicants must meet the physical and mental standards necessary for safe driving. Medical conditions affecting driving ability must be disclosed.

4. **Compliance with Legal Requirements**: Applicants must not have outstanding suspensions or revocations on their driving record.

Application Tips

- Double-check that all documents are current and valid. Expired or incomplete documents will not be accepted.

- Ensure that your name matches across all documents to avoid discrepancies.

- If you are unsure about document requirements, visit the Utah DMV website or contact a local office for clarification.

Meeting these requirements is essential to successfully apply for a driver's license. Proper preparation ensures a smooth and efficient application process.

Fees and Timelines

When applying for a driver's license in Utah, understanding the associated fees and timelines is essential for proper planning. This section provides a detailed overview of the costs and timeframes involved in obtaining your license.

Fees Associated with Obtaining a License

The Utah DMV charges a variety of fees depending on the type of license or permit being applied for. Below is a breakdown of the most common costs:

1. **Learner's Permit**: The application fee for a learner's permit is $19. This fee covers the knowledge test, vision test, and the issuance of the permit.

2. **Standard Driver's License**: The fee for a standard driver's license is $52. This includes the cost of the road test and the issuance of the license. Renewal fees are $25.

3. **Commercial Driver's License (CDL)**: CDL application fees vary based on the class and endorsements. The base fee is $60, with additional costs for endorsements such as hazardous materials or passenger vehicles.

4. **Motorcycle Endorsement**: Adding a motorcycle endorsement to an existing license costs $18. A separate motorcycle permit costs $15.

5. **State ID Card**: For individuals not seeking a driver's license, the fee for a state identification card is $23.

6. **Duplicate or Replacement License**: If your license is lost, stolen, or damaged, the fee for a replacement is $23.

Additional Fees

- **Testing Fees**: If you fail the written or road test, a retesting fee of $10 applies for each attempt.

- **Late Renewal Penalty**: Renewing an expired license incurs a $10 penalty.

- **Vision Correction Restriction Removal**: If you've had corrective surgery and wish to remove a vision restriction from your license, a $20 fee is required.

Timelines for the Licensing Process

The time it takes to complete the licensing process depends on individual preparedness and the specific type of license being pursued. Below is an estimated timeline for each step:

1. **Preparation Phase**: Gathering required documents, completing driver education, and practicing driving can take anywhere from a few weeks to several months, depending on your availability and readiness.

2. **Learner's Permit**: After passing the knowledge and vision tests, you will receive your permit on the same day. The permit is valid for one year, allowing ample time to practice driving.

3. **Road Test Scheduling**: Road test appointments at the DMV may have a wait time of 1-4 weeks, depending on demand. Booking early can help minimize delays.

4. **License Issuance**: Once you pass the road test, your license is typically issued immediately. Temporary paper licenses are provided while the physical card is mailed, which can take 7-10 business days to arrive.

5. **Renewals**: License renewals can often be completed online or in person. The processing time for online renewals is usually 3-5 business days.

Tips for Managing Costs and Time

- **Plan Ahead**: Schedule your road test and gather documents early to avoid delays.

- **Budget Wisely**: Be aware of all associated fees and set aside the necessary funds.

- **Check DMV Schedules**: Visit the Utah DMV website for updated timelines and fee structures.

By understanding the fees and timelines involved, you can navigate the licensing process efficiently and avoid unnecessary expenses or delays.

Common Pitfalls and How to Avoid Them

The process of obtaining a driver's license in Utah can be straightforward if you are well-prepared. However, many applicants encounter obstacles that delay or complicate the process. This section highlights eight common pitfalls and offers practical tips for avoiding them.

1. Incomplete Documentation

One of the most frequent mistakes applicants make is arriving at the DMV without all required documents. Missing or expired documents can result in rescheduled appointments and wasted time.

How to Avoid:

- Use a checklist to verify that you have all necessary documents, such as proof of identity, Social Security number, and proof of residency.

- Double-check that all documents are current and match the information on your application.

2. Failure to Prepare for the Knowledge Test

Many applicants underestimate the difficulty of the written knowledge test, leading to failed attempts and retesting fees.

How to Avoid:

- Study the Utah Driver Handbook thoroughly.

- Take online practice tests to familiarize yourself with the format and types of questions.

- Focus on areas where you struggle and review them multiple times.

3. Insufficient Driving Practice

A lack of hands-on driving experience often leads to failure in the road test. Nervousness and unfamiliarity with driving maneuvers can hinder performance.

How to Avoid:

- Complete the required 40 hours of supervised driving practice, including 10 hours at night.

- Practice specific skills, such as parallel parking, lane changes, and three-point turns.

- Use DMV road test checklists to ensure you're prepared.

4. Scheduling Delays

Procrastination in scheduling the road test or gathering documents can lead to long waits, especially during busy seasons.

How to Avoid:

- Schedule your road test as soon as you're eligible.

- Keep track of deadlines and make appointments early.

5. Ignoring Vision Requirements

Failing the vision test can disqualify you from obtaining a license. Applicants often overlook this requirement until it's too late.

How to Avoid:

- Visit an optometrist for a vision check before your DMV appointment.

- Wear corrective lenses if required and ensure your prescription is up-to-date.

6. Overlooking Fees

Unexpected fees can catch applicants off guard, especially if they need to retake tests or replace lost documents.

How to Avoid:

- Familiarize yourself with all applicable fees, including testing, licensing, and renewal costs.

- Bring sufficient funds or a credit card to cover these expenses.

7. Misunderstanding Road Test Expectations

Failing the road test often results from a lack of understanding of what evaluators are looking for. Common errors include failing to check blind spots, improper lane usage, and incomplete stops.

How to Avoid:

- Review the DMV's road test requirements and guidelines.

- Practice with a licensed driver who can provide constructive feedback.

- Remain calm and focused during the test, following all instructions carefully.

8. Ignoring Provisional License Restrictions

New drivers, especially those under 18, sometimes violate the restrictions of their provisional licenses, leading to penalties or suspension.

How to Avoid:

- Familiarize yourself with the restrictions, such as limits on night-time driving and the number of passengers allowed.

- Adhere strictly to these rules until the restrictions are lifted.

Additional Tips for Success

1. **Arrive Early**: Showing up late for your appointment can result in rescheduling. Plan to arrive at least 15 minutes early.

2. **Check DMV Hours**: Ensure the DMV office is open on the day of your visit and confirm any holiday closures.

3. **Dress Appropriately**: Wear comfortable clothing and shoes suitable for driving.

4. **Stay Informed**: Regularly check the Utah DMV website for updates on requirements, fees, and testing procedures.

Chapter 2

Exploring Traffic Laws of Utah

Utah's traffic laws are designed to ensure the safety of all road users and promote responsible driving behaviour. These laws encompass general rules applicable to all drivers as well as specific regulations tailored to the unique needs of the state. Adhering to these laws not only helps reduce accidents but also fosters a culture of respect and accountability on the roads.

Utah's driving laws cover a broad range of areas, including speed limits, right of way, parking regulations, and DUI offenses. Drivers are expected to understand and comply with these laws to maintain their driving privileges. The state also mandates strict adherence to traffic signals, signs, and road markings to facilitate orderly traffic flow.

Recent legislative updates have introduced new measures to address emerging challenges, such as distracted driving and increased urban traffic. The Utah Department of Transportation works closely with law enforcement to ensure compliance and promote road safety through educational campaigns and enforcement initiatives. By staying informed about these regulations, drivers can contribute to safer roads and avoid legal consequences.

General Driving Laws in Utah

Utah enforces a set of general driving laws applicable to all motorists, emphasizing safety and accountability. These laws include adhering to speed limits, obeying traffic signals, and maintaining proper vehicle registration and insurance. Understanding these foundational rules is essential for anyone operating a vehicle within the state.

Drivers must always yield to emergency vehicles displaying flashing lights and using sirens. When an emergency vehicle approaches, motorists are required to pull over to the nearest curb or edge of the roadway and remain stopped until the vehicle passes. Failure to comply can result in severe penalties.

The use of seat belts is mandatory for all passengers in a vehicle, regardless of their seating position. Utah law also requires child restraint systems for young passengers based on their age, weight, and height. These measures are critical for reducing injuries during accidents.

Drivers are prohibited from using handheld devices while operating a vehicle. Texting, calling, or any activity that distracts from driving is considered a violation of Utah's distracted driving laws. Hands-free options are encouraged to minimize distractions and improve focus on the road.

Proper lane usage is another cornerstone of Utah's driving laws. Motorists must signal appropriately when changing lanes and avoid weaving between traffic. Additionally, vehicles traveling at slower speeds must use the right lane to allow faster-moving traffic to pass safely on the left.

Utah enforces strict DUI regulations, prohibiting drivers from operating a vehicle with a blood alcohol concentration (BAC) of 0.05% or higher. Offenders face severe penalties, including fines, license suspension, and mandatory participation in educational programs.

Drivers are also obligated to stop at all railroad crossings when signals indicate an approaching train. Ignoring these signals can lead to catastrophic accidents and legal repercussions. Similarly, school zones require reduced speeds during designated hours to protect children and pedestrians.

Specific Laws Unique to Utah

Utah has enacted several traffic laws tailored to address the state's unique geographical, cultural, and environmental factors. Understanding these specific regulations is crucial for both residents and visitors to navigate Utah's roads responsibly.

One distinctive law in Utah involves snow tire requirements during winter months. From November 1 to March 31, vehicles traveling in certain mountainous regions must be equipped with snow tires or chains to ensure safe driving on icy or snowy roads. Violating this law can result in fines and increased risk of accidents.

Utah also has unique provisions for off-highway vehicles (OHVs). Drivers of ATVs, snowmobiles, and other OHVs must adhere to specific rules, including obtaining proper permits and avoiding restricted areas. These regulations are designed to protect natural landscapes and ensure the safety of both OHV operators and other road users.

In urban areas, Utah enforces strict idling restrictions to reduce air pollution. Vehicles are not allowed to idle for more than two minutes under most circumstances. Exceptions are made for extreme weather conditions and certain commercial vehicles, but violators may face fines.

Another unique regulation pertains to the state's HOV (High-Occupancy Vehicle) lanes. These lanes are reserved for vehicles with two or more occupants during peak hours. Solo drivers can use HOV lanes only if they purchase a Clean Vehicle Pass for qualifying low-emission vehicles.

Utah's "Move Over" law requires drivers to change lanes or reduce speed when approaching stationary emergency vehicles, tow trucks, or maintenance vehicles displaying flashing lights. This law aims to protect workers and first responders performing duties on the roadside.

Cyclists in Utah benefit from specific protections under state law. Motorists must provide at least three feet of clearance when passing a bicycle. Additionally, cyclists are allowed to use the full lane if necessary for safety, such as when avoiding obstacles or navigating narrow roads.

In terms of wildlife conservation, Utah imposes strict penalties for littering and feeding wildlife from vehicles. These practices disrupt ecosystems and can lead to dangerous encounters between animals and road users.

Utah also regulates vehicle modifications, such as window tinting and exhaust systems. Tinted windows must allow at least 43% light transmission, and modified exhausts must comply with noise ordinances. Violations can result in fines and required modifications to bring vehicles into compliance.

Legal Responsibilities of Utah Drivers

Being a licensed driver in Utah comes with significant legal responsibilities that extend beyond merely following traffic laws. Drivers are expected to uphold standards that ensure the safety of themselves, their passengers, and others on the road.

One primary responsibility is maintaining valid vehicle insurance. Utah requires all drivers to carry minimum liability insurance coverage, which includes $25,000 for bodily injury per person, $65,000 for bodily injury per accident, and $15,000 for property damage. Proof of insurance must be presented during traffic stops, accidents, and vehicle registration.

Drivers involved in accidents have a legal obligation to stop and provide assistance if necessary. They must exchange information with other parties involved, including name, address, driver's license number, and insurance details. For accidents resulting in significant damage, injury, or death, drivers must also report the incident to law enforcement.

Utah law mandates that drivers address traffic citations promptly. Ignoring tickets or failing to appear in court can result in additional fines, license suspension, or even arrest warrants. It is the driver's responsibility to either pay the fine or contest the citation within the designated timeframe.

Keeping vehicles in roadworthy condition is another critical responsibility. Drivers must ensure that their vehicles meet safety standards, including functioning brakes, lights, and tires. Regular vehicle inspections help identify and address potential issues that could compromise safety.

Drivers are also required to renew their licenses before expiration. Utah provides a grace period for renewals, but driving with an expired license is a violation of state law. The renewal process includes updating personal information and, in some cases, passing a vision test.

Adhering to the rules of the road extends to interactions with vulnerable road users, such as pedestrians and cyclists. Utah drivers must yield the right of way to pedestrians in crosswalks and exercise caution when sharing the road with cyclists.

Finally, drivers are expected to be aware of their physical and mental fitness to operate a vehicle. Driving under the influence of alcohol, drugs, or medications that impair judgment is strictly prohibited and carries severe penalties. Similarly, drivers experiencing medical conditions that affect their ability to drive safely must inform the DMV and comply with any restrictions.

Recent Legislative Updates

In recent years, Utah has implemented several legislative changes aimed at enhancing road safety and addressing emerging challenges in transportation. These updates reflect the state's commitment to adapting its traffic laws to evolving societal and technological needs. Staying informed about these changes is crucial for all drivers to ensure compliance and avoid penalties.

One significant update involves distracted driving laws. Utah has intensified its efforts to combat distracted driving by imposing stricter penalties for the use of handheld devices while driving. As of the latest legislation, drivers caught texting or engaging in other distracting activities face higher fines and potential license points. The state encourages the use of hands-free devices to minimize distractions and improve road safety.

Another notable change pertains to speed limits in urban areas. To address the increasing number of pedestrian accidents, Utah has reduced speed limits in certain residential and school zones. These adjustments aim to create safer environments for pedestrians and cyclists, particularly in densely populated areas.

Utah has also introduced measures to regulate autonomous vehicles (AVs). As AV technology becomes more prevalent, the state has established guidelines for testing and operating self-driving cars on public roads. These regulations include requirements for safety features, liability insurance, and real-time monitoring systems to ensure the safety of all road users.

In response to environmental concerns, Utah has expanded its idling restrictions to reduce vehicle emissions. The updated laws impose stricter limits on idling time, particularly in urban areas with high pollution levels. Exceptions are made for extreme weather conditions and vehicles used for emergency services, but violators may face increased fines.

The state has also revised its DUI laws to include stricter penalties for repeat offenders. Drivers with multiple DUI convictions now face longer license suspensions, mandatory participation in rehabilitation programs, and the installation of ignition interlock devices. These measures aim to deter impaired driving and enhance public safety.

Utah's "Move Over" law has been extended to include disabled vehicles. Drivers are required to change lanes or reduce speed when approaching not only emergency and maintenance vehicles but also stationary vehicles with hazard lights activated. This update seeks to protect stranded motorists and roadside assistance workers from potential collisions.

crosswalks and intersections. Drivers are now required to come to a complete stop, not just yield, for pedestrians entering or within a marked crosswalk. This adjustment emphasizes the importance of pedestrian safety and reduces the risk of accidents in high-traffic areas. Failure to comply with these regulations can result in significant fines and penalties.

Recent legislation has also focused on improving road safety for motorcyclists. Utah has adopted lane-filtering laws, allowing motorcyclists to navigate between lanes of stopped or slow-moving vehicles in certain conditions. This change aims to reduce congestion and improve safety for motorcyclists by minimizing their exposure to rear-end collisions.

The state has also made updates to its driver education requirements. To better prepare new drivers, Utah has mandated additional hours of behind-the-wheel training and enhanced the curriculum to include lessons on distracted driving, defensive driving techniques, and the responsibilities of sharing the road with cyclists and pedestrians.

Lastly, Utah has addressed the increasing use of electric vehicles (EVs) by updating its registration and tax policies. EV owners are now required to pay a road usage fee in lieu of traditional gas taxes, ensuring that all drivers contribute fairly to the maintenance of Utah's roads and infrastructure.

Speed Limits and Speeding Penalties

Speed limits in Utah are strictly enforced to promote the safety of all road users. They vary depending on the type of road and location, and it is essential for drivers to understand the specific speed limits applicable to different areas.

- **Urban Areas and Residential Zones**: In most urban and residential areas, the speed limit is typically set at 25 miles per hour (mph). These areas often include schools, parks, and neighbourhoods where pedestrian activity is higher, and slower speeds are necessary for safety.

- **Business Districts**: In commercial areas, the speed limit is generally 25 to 35 mph. These limits are designed to account for heavy pedestrian traffic and frequent stops for vehicles entering and exiting businesses.

- **Rural Roads**: Outside urban areas, speed limits are often higher, with speeds ranging between 45 and 55 mph. However, caution is necessary as some rural roads can be narrower or less maintained, requiring drivers to reduce speed as needed.

- **Interstate Highways**: The speed limit on Utah's interstate highways typically ranges from 65 mph to 75 mph, depending on the region. In some more remote areas, drivers may encounter speed limits as high as 80 mph. These higher limits apply to roads designed for faster travel and longer distances.

- **School Zones**: In school zones, the speed limit is typically reduced to 20 mph during school hours. Drivers must always watch for signs indicating reduced speeds and be prepared to slow down, especially when children are present near the road.

Penalties for speeding in Utah can vary depending on how far over the speed limit the driver is traveling. Fines are usually assessed for violations, and the severity increases with the amount by which the speed limit is exceeded. Speeding 1-10 mph over the limit typically results in a small fine, while speeding more than 20 mph over the limit can result in higher fines, increased penalties, or even a suspension of the driver's license. Additionally, speeding violations may lead to points added to the driver's record, which can eventually lead to higher insurance premiums or a suspended license if too many points accumulate.

Right of Way Rules

Understanding right of way rules is crucial for ensuring safe and smooth traffic flow. These rules dictate who has the right to proceed first in different driving situations, preventing confusion and reducing the likelihood of accidents. Below are the primary rules for determining the right of way in Utah:

- **At Intersections without Signs or Signals**: When approaching an intersection without traffic control signals or signs, the driver must yield to vehicles coming from the right.

- **At Stop Signs**: A driver approaching a stop sign must come to a complete stop and yield to any vehicles or pedestrians already in or approaching the intersection. When two vehicles arrive at a stop sign simultaneously, the vehicle on the right has the right of way.

- **At Yield Signs**: A driver approaching a yield sign must slow down and yield to oncoming traffic or pedestrians. The driver should only proceed when it is safe to do so without impeding other road users.

- **Turning Left or Right**: When turning left, the driver must yield to all oncoming traffic, including pedestrians in crosswalks. Similarly, when turning right, drivers must yield to pedestrians in crosswalks and cyclists who may be approaching.

- **Roundabouts**: In a roundabout, vehicles inside the roundabout have the right of way. Drivers entering the roundabout must yield to traffic already circulating.

- **Pedestrian Crosswalks**: Drivers must always yield to pedestrians who are crossing the road at marked or unmarked crosswalks, whether or not the pedestrian is on a signalized crosswalk.

- **Emergency Vehicles**: When an emergency vehicle with flashing lights approaches, all vehicles must pull over to the right side of the road and stop to allow the emergency vehicle to pass.

- **At T-intersections**: When coming to a T-intersection, the driver on the through road has the right of way. The driver on the road that ends must yield to oncoming traffic.

These rules are designed to prevent accidents and ensure that traffic flows in a predictable and safe manner. Failure to adhere to right of way rules can lead to accidents and legal consequences.

Laws Regarding Pedestrians and Cyclists

Utah law includes several important provisions designed to ensure the safety of pedestrians and cyclists. These laws protect vulnerable road users and outline the responsibilities of both drivers and pedestrians/cyclists. Below are the key laws related to pedestrians and cyclists:

- **Pedestrian Right of Way**: Drivers must yield to pedestrians at marked and unmarked crosswalks. Pedestrians have the right of way when they are legally crossing the street at these locations.

- **Pedestrian Crosswalks**: It is illegal for drivers to pass a vehicle that is stopped at a crosswalk in order to allow pedestrians to cross. Additionally, drivers must not block crosswalks with their vehicles.

- **School Zones**: In school zones, drivers must reduce speed and be extra cautious, as children are more likely to cross the street in these areas. Pedestrians have the right of way, especially when crossing in school zones or near school bus stops.

- **Cyclist Rights**: Cyclists in Utah have the same rights and responsibilities as drivers of motor vehicles. Cyclists are required to obey all traffic signals, signs, and rules of the road, and must use designated bike lanes when available. In areas without bike lanes, cyclists should ride as close to the right edge of the road as safely possible.

- **Cycling on Sidewalks**: Cyclists are not permitted to ride on sidewalks in some areas. Local ordinances may vary, so cyclists should be aware of specific regulations regarding sidewalk cycling.

- **Helmet Laws**: Cyclists under the age of 18 are required to wear a helmet while riding on public roads, but this is not mandated for adult cyclists.

- **Pedestrian and Cyclist Impairment**: Pedestrians and cyclists who are impaired due to alcohol or drugs may be subject to the same penalties as motor vehicle drivers. Both groups should be cautious when under the influence of substances that affect judgment and coordination.

These laws are in place to protect vulnerable road users, promote safety, and reduce the potential for accidents involving pedestrians and cyclists.

Parking Regulations

Parking regulations in Utah are designed to maintain order on the roads and ensure that parking spaces are used efficiently and legally. Here is a summary of both legal and illegal parking practices in Utah:

Legal Parking:

- Parking is allowed in designated parking spaces or along streets where parking is permitted.
- Drivers must park within the lines of marked parking spaces.
- It is legal to park on the right side of the street, in the direction of traffic flow, unless otherwise posted.
- Disabled parking spaces are reserved for individuals with disabilities, and parking in these spaces without the proper permit is illegal.

Illegal Parking:

- **Blocking Driveways**: It is illegal to park in front of a driveway or block access to private property.
- **Fire Hydrants**: Parking within 15 feet of a fire hydrant is prohibited, ensuring that emergency services have access to the hydrant in case of an emergency.
- **No Parking Zones**: Parking in areas marked with "No Parking" signs, such as areas near intersections, crosswalks, and bus stops, is not permitted.

- **Double Parking**: Double parking, or parking alongside another vehicle that is already parked, is prohibited.
- **Handicapped Spaces**: Parking in designated handicapped spaces without the proper permit is a violation and can result in fines.

Violating parking regulations can result in fines, towing of the vehicle, and in some cases, points on the driver's license.

Driving Under the Influence

In Utah, driving under the influence (DUI) of alcohol or drugs is considered a serious offense. The legal blood alcohol concentration (BAC) limit for drivers over the age of 21 is 0.05%. For drivers under 21, the BAC limit is 0.00%. Utah law also prohibits driving under the influence of controlled substances, including marijuana, prescription medications, and illicit drugs.

Penalties for DUI include fines, license suspension, mandatory alcohol or drug education classes, and possibly jail time, depending on the severity of the offense and whether it is a first-time or repeat offense. DUI offenders may also be required to install an ignition interlock device (IID) in their vehicles, which prevents the vehicle from starting if alcohol is detected on the driver's breath.

In addition to the legal consequences, DUI convictions carry long-term consequences, including higher insurance premiums, a criminal record, and a significant impact on employment opportunities.

Understanding Traffic Cameras and Enforcement

Traffic cameras in Utah play a crucial role in enforcing traffic laws and improving road safety. These cameras are typically placed at intersections, along highways, and in areas where traffic violations are common. They are used to capture violations such as running red lights, speeding, and driving through stop signs.

Traffic cameras work by detecting a vehicle's movement and triggering a photo or video when a violation occurs. For instance, a red-light camera is activated when a vehicle passes through an intersection after the light has turned red. Similarly, speed cameras measure the speed of passing vehicles and capture an image of those exceeding the speed limit.

The penalties associated with traffic camera violations vary by the type of violation. Typically, fines are issued to the registered owner of the vehicle. In the case of red light or speed camera violations, drivers can expect a fine along with possible points added to their driving record, which can lead to higher insurance premiums or even suspension of their driver's license if too many points accumulate.

These cameras contribute significantly to reducing accidents and traffic violations by providing a way to catch offenders who might otherwise go unnoticed. They also serve as a deterrent to unsafe driving behaviours.

Driving Etiquette

Driving etiquette is essential to maintaining a courteous and safe driving environment. Common courtesy on the road reduces the potential for accidents, minimizes road rage, and promotes cooperation among drivers. Here are some key aspects of driving etiquette that all motorists should adhere to.

First, signalling is one of the most basic yet important aspects of driving etiquette. Always signal your intentions, whether you're changing lanes, merging, or making a turn. This lets other drivers know your plans and helps them anticipate your actions, contributing to smoother traffic flow and reducing the risk of collisions. Failing to signal can cause confusion and lead to accidents, especially in busy traffic conditions.

Yielding to pedestrians is another crucial part of driving etiquette. Pedestrians, especially in crosswalks or school zones, have the right of way. Be patient and wait for them to cross safely before proceeding. Stopping for pedestrians not only ensures safety but also reflects good driving behaviour and respect for others. Similarly, be mindful of cyclists who are sharing the road. Cyclists have the same rights as motorists, and it's important to give them enough space when passing or turning.

Blocking intersections is another behaviour that should be avoided at all costs. When the light turns red, make sure your vehicle is not obstructing the intersection. This can prevent gridlock and allow other vehicles to move through when the light changes. Blocking intersections is not only inconsiderate but also illegal in many jurisdictions.

Driving with patience and avoiding aggressive behaviours, such as tailgating or honking unnecessarily, is vital for maintaining peace on the road. If you are in a hurry, try to be understanding of other drivers' limitations and remember that your impatience can cause accidents or escalate conflicts. Furthermore, never engage in road rage by yelling or making obscene gestures at other drivers.

Lastly, avoid distractions while driving. This includes refraining from texting, using your phone for non-essential purposes, or eating while driving. Distractions significantly increase the risk of accidents, and focusing entirely on the road is crucial for your safety and the safety of others.

Special Considerations for New Drivers

For new or inexperienced drivers, the road can feel overwhelming at times. Building confidence behind the wheel takes time, practice, and awareness of your surroundings. Here are some key tips for new drivers to help them navigate the challenges they might face.

Start by practicing in low-traffic areas, such as parking lots or quiet streets, where you can gain control of your vehicle and build comfort without the added pressure of heavy traffic. Gradually progress to busier roads as your skills improve. The more practice you get, the more confident and comfortable you will feel behind the wheel.

Pay close attention to traffic signs, signals, and lane markings. Being able to quickly identify these will help you anticipate actions, such as when to stop, slow down, or make turns. You should always follow traffic laws strictly, even if other drivers are not obeying them. Safety should be your top priority, and driving safely is more important than keeping up with traffic.

Take time to adjust your mirrors, seat, and steering wheel before driving. Proper visibility and comfort will help you maintain better control of the vehicle. Practice defensive driving techniques, such as maintaining a safe following distance and staying aware of other vehicles around you. This will help you react to unexpected situations more effectively.

Don't rush when making decisions on the road. It is better to wait a few extra seconds than to make a risky move that could endanger yourself or others. Building good habits, like checking your blind spots and using turn signals regularly, will make you a more skilled driver over time.

Finally, take a defensive driving course if possible. These courses can teach valuable techniques and strategies for staying safe on the road and handling unexpected situations.

Chapter 3

Rules of the Road

Utah has specific rules of the road designed to ensure the safety of all drivers, pedestrians, and cyclists. These rules provide a framework that allows traffic to flow smoothly and safely, minimizing the risk of accidents and ensuring that every road user knows what is expected of them.

One of the most important aspects of Utah's road rules is the adherence to speed limits. Speed limits vary based on the area and road type, and drivers must always follow posted speed signs. Additionally, yielding the right of way is crucial in preventing accidents. Utah law requires drivers to yield to pedestrians at crosswalks and follow the rules governing who has the right to proceed at intersections, as well as when merging or changing lanes.

Another critical element of Utah's rules is the prohibition of driving under the influence of alcohol or drugs, with strict penalties for offenders. Drivers must always wear seat belts, and child passengers are required by law to use proper restraints, depending on their age and size.

Proper lane usage is another key component of Utah's driving rules. Drivers must maintain their lane of travel unless it is necessary to change lanes for a legal manoeuvre, such as turning or overtaking another vehicle. The rules for lane usage are designed to avoid confusion and ensure that traffic moves efficiently, particularly on highways and busy city streets.

Finally, safe driving practices, such as using turn signals, observing traffic signs, and following all posted road regulations, contribute to a predictable and safe driving environment for all. Drivers must also be prepared to adjust to road conditions and the behaviour of other road users to maintain a high level of safety.

Lane Usage and Changing Lanes

Lane usage is a critical part of safe driving. Proper lane usage ensures that traffic flows smoothly and reduces the risk of accidents. The lane that a driver chooses should be based on the direction they intend to go and the speed at which they need to travel.

On multi-lane roads, the left lane is generally reserved for vehicles that are traveling at higher speeds or overtaking slower vehicles. The right lane is typically used for normal driving, especially for vehicles that are not in a hurry. Drivers should avoid staying in the left lane unless they are actively passing another vehicle. It is important to remember that lingering in the left lane without a valid reason can impede the flow of traffic and lead to frustration or unsafe passing manoeuvres from other drivers.

Changing lanes requires careful consideration. Before changing lanes, a driver must always check their mirrors and blind spots to ensure that the lane is clear of other vehicles, cyclists, or pedestrians. It is also important to use your turn signals to indicate your intention to other drivers. This helps to prevent confusion and reduces the risk of accidents during lane changes.

When changing lanes, the driver should make the move smoothly without abrupt steering, and they should avoid cutting off other vehicles. The manoeuvre should be performed only when necessary and should never be done in areas where lane changes are prohibited, such as in intersections or near exits. Always ensure there is enough space in the next lane before making the change and avoid aggressive or hasty lane switching, which can endanger you and other road users.

Additionally, when entering a highway from an entrance ramp, it is critical to signal your intent to merge and adjust your speed to match the flow of traffic. This helps prevent accidents and ensures a smooth merge without causing disruptions to other drivers.

Proper lane discipline is not just about following laws; it is about ensuring the safety of all road users. Drivers should be aware of the different lane rules for different types of roads, such as highways, city streets, or residential areas. Practicing good lane usage habits, such as staying in the correct lane and changing lanes safely, will help you avoid accidents and keep traffic flowing smoothly.

Passing Other Vehicles

Passing other vehicles is a common manoeuvre that drivers must perform when slower traffic is impeding their progress. However, it is important to pass other vehicles safely to ensure the safety of both yourself and the other road users. The following guidelines detail the rules and best practices for passing other vehicles.

- **Ensure a Clear Path**: Before attempting to pass another vehicle, always ensure that the road ahead is clear of obstacles and other vehicles. Look ahead for any oncoming traffic, and only pass when there is enough space and time to complete the manoeuvre without putting yourself or others in danger.

- **Use the Left Lane**: In most cases, passing other vehicles should be done in the left lane. Always check your mirrors and blind spots before moving into the left lane to ensure there are no vehicles behind you that may be attempting to pass.

- **Signal Your Intent**: Always signal your intention to pass another vehicle by using your turn signal. This alerts other drivers to your movements, which is especially important when passing on multi-lane roads or highways.

- **Pass Safely and Swiftly**: When passing, do so quickly but safely. Maintain a steady speed and avoid excessive acceleration or cutting off the vehicle you are passing. Once you have passed, ensure that you have sufficient space to return to your original lane before signalling and steering back.

- **Do Not Pass in Dangerous Areas**: Avoid passing other vehicles in areas where it is illegal or unsafe to do so. For example, do not pass vehicles in curves, on hills, or near intersections where your visibility may be limited. Passing is also prohibited in areas marked with solid yellow lines, which indicate no-passing zones.

- **Avoid Passing Large Vehicles**: When passing large vehicles such as trucks or buses, exercise extra caution. These vehicles have large blind spots, and the driver may not be able to see you. Always ensure there is a clear gap between you and the vehicle you are passing, and wait until you are far enough ahead to safely return to the right lane.

- **Don't Pass on the Right**: In Utah, as in most states, passing other vehicles on the right is only allowed when there are two or more lanes in the same direction of travel and it is safe to do so. Never pass on the right when the vehicle ahead is turning left or in situations where it is illegal to do so.

Intersections and Turns

Intersections and turns are high-risk areas for accidents, as they involve multiple vehicles or road users interacting at the same time. The following guidelines outline the proper procedures for navigating intersections and making turns to ensure safety.

- **At Intersections Without Signals**: When approaching an intersection without traffic signals, drivers must yield to vehicles coming from the right. Always come to a complete stop at a stop sign and give the right of way to any vehicles or pedestrians already in or approaching the intersection.

- **Turning Left or Right**: When making a turn, it is important to signal your intentions well in advance. For left turns, always yield to oncoming traffic and pedestrians. When turning right, yield to pedestrians in crosswalks. Always make turns slowly and check for any other vehicles or pedestrians in your path before proceeding.

- **U-Turns**: U-turns are generally allowed in Utah, but drivers should only make them where it is safe and legal. Ensure that no oncoming traffic or pedestrians will be affected by the turn. Always check for posted signs that may prohibit U-turns, such as in certain intersections or near curves.

- **Traffic Signals**: At signalized intersections, obey all traffic signals. If the light is red, stop and remain stopped until the light turns green. If the light turns yellow as you approach, proceed with caution, but do not attempt to speed through the intersection.

- **Pedestrian Crosswalks**: Always yield to pedestrians in marked crosswalks. If there is no crosswalk, yield to pedestrians as they have the right of way, especially in residential areas or school zones. Never block the crosswalk with your vehicle.

- **Left Turns at Intersections**: When making a left turn at an intersection, always signal in advance and position your vehicle in the leftmost lane. Yield to oncoming vehicles and wait for a clear gap in traffic before completing the turn.

- **Roundabouts and Traffic Circles**: When entering a roundabout or traffic circle, yield to the vehicles already in the circle. Wait for a safe gap and enter when you can do so without interfering with the flow of traffic.

Navigating intersections and making turns safely requires awareness, patience, and adherence to traffic laws. Always signal your intentions and be prepared to yield to other road users as necessary.

Roundabouts

Roundabouts are circular intersections designed to keep traffic moving smoothly while reducing the likelihood of accidents. They are becoming more common in Utah and other states due to their safety and efficiency. However, navigating roundabouts correctly requires drivers to follow specific rules and guidelines to ensure a safe and smooth experience for everyone on the road.

Roundabouts are designed to keep traffic flowing continuously, and they typically have one-way traffic that moves in a counter clockwise direction in the United States. The key to safely navigating roundabouts is to yield to traffic already in the circle and enter when there is a safe gap.

Before entering a roundabout, drivers should slow down and be prepared to yield to any vehicles already in the roundabout. These vehicles have the right of way, and you should wait for a safe opportunity to enter. Look for any pedestrians or cyclists who may be crossing or waiting to cross, as they also have the right of way.

When approaching a roundabout, look for signs that indicate the number of lanes and any specific instructions for lane usage. If the roundabout has multiple lanes, choose the appropriate lane for your destination, keeping in mind that you may need to exit from the right lane. Make sure to signal your intentions as you approach the exit and check for other vehicles.

Once in the roundabout, maintain a steady speed and stay in your lane. If you miss your exit or need to change lanes, continue around the circle until you reach the correct exit. Avoid making abrupt lane changes or sudden stops within the roundabout, as this can cause confusion and accidents.

In some cases, roundabouts may have pedestrian crossings located just before or after the circular area. Always be on the lookout for pedestrians, especially in busy areas where they may be crossing the road.

Railroad Crossings

Railroad crossings are potentially dangerous areas where roads intersect with railway tracks. In Utah, as in many other states, drivers must take special care when approaching and crossing railroad tracks. Adhering to the proper safety procedures at these crossings can prevent accidents and save lives.

Approaching a railroad crossing requires caution, especially when approaching at high speeds or on unfamiliar roads. Always be on the lookout for warning signs indicating the presence of a railroad crossing, such as flashing red lights, bells, or gates. These signals are in place to alert drivers that a train is approaching.

When approaching a railroad crossing, always slow down and be prepared to stop. Never attempt to cross the tracks when the warning lights are flashing, or when the gates are down. If the lights are flashing or the gate is lowered, wait for it to rise or stop before proceeding. You should also stop at a railroad crossing if there is no visible train and the signals are activated, as trains can approach at unexpected times.

Be aware that some railroad crossings do not have gates or flashing lights but are still regulated by stop signs. In these cases, come to a complete stop and look both ways before crossing the tracks. Always listen for any approaching trains and make sure the tracks are clear before proceeding.

If you are stopped at a railroad crossing, never attempt to drive around lowered gates. It is also important to remember that trains can take a long time to pass, so remain patient and wait for the crossing to clear before proceeding. If you are caught on the tracks with a train approaching, immediately exit your vehicle and move to a safe location.

In some cases, railroad crossings may be equipped with pedestrian crossings. Always yield to pedestrians in these areas, especially if they are waiting to cross the tracks.

Navigating Construction Zones

Construction zones are areas where roadwork is taking place and are often marked by warning signs, cones, and barriers. These zones can present a variety of hazards for drivers, including narrowed lanes, uneven surfaces, and potential disruptions to normal traffic flow. It is critical to exercise caution and follow the appropriate guidelines to ensure safety when navigating through construction zones.

Obey Detour Signs and Traffic Control Devices: When driving through a construction zone, it is important to follow all detour signs and traffic control devices. These signs are placed to guide drivers around the construction area or to direct traffic in a manner that ensures the safety of both workers and drivers. Ignoring detours or attempting to navigate through closed-off areas can lead to accidents or traffic violations.

Reduced Speed Limits: Construction zones typically have reduced speed limits, which are clearly posted. These lower speeds are intended to give drivers more time to react to any sudden changes in road conditions and to protect construction workers who may be working close to traffic. It is crucial to obey these speed limits, as failure to do so can result in fines or, more dangerously, accidents. Even if no workers are visible, the reduced speed limit should be maintained to ensure the safety of the site.

Be Alert for Workers and Equipment: Construction zones are often active with workers, heavy machinery, and other vehicles. It is important to remain alert and watch for workers who may be in close proximity to moving traffic. Slow down as you approach construction zones, and be prepared to stop if necessary. Workers may be working in lanes that are open to traffic, and construction vehicles may enter or exit the area unexpectedly.

Use Turn Signals and Avoid Lane Changes: Construction zones typically have marked lanes and boundaries that should be followed. Lane changes in construction zones are often restricted, and failure to adhere to lane markings can disrupt the flow of traffic and endanger workers. Always use your turn signals when changing lanes and ensure that you are not crossing into restricted areas.

Stay Focused and Minimize Distractions: Construction zones can be complex, and drivers should avoid distractions such as texting or using a mobile phone while passing through these areas. Staying focused on the road ahead, adhering to posted instructions, and being mindful of the construction workers' safety will help ensure that both drivers and workers remain protected.

Keep a Safe Distance from Construction Vehicles: Maintain a safe distance between your vehicle and construction vehicles, as they may stop suddenly or change directions without warning. These vehicles often have limited visibility, and keeping a safe distance allows you to react appropriately to any unexpected movements.

Watch for Changing Road Conditions: Construction zones may have shifting road conditions, such as new lane markings, uneven surfaces, or changes in traffic flow. Stay alert for changes in the road, and be prepared to adjust your speed and position accordingly.

Driving Situations: Who Has the Right of Way?

In certain driving situations, knowing who has the right of way or what actions should be taken is crucial for maintaining the flow of traffic and preventing accidents. Below are 12 real-life examples of driving situations, where the right of way should be observed, along with the proper actions that should be taken.

1. **Roundabouts**: When entering a roundabout, vehicles already inside the roundabout have the right of way. Drivers must yield to vehicles already circulating before entering. To safely navigate, wait for a clear gap and enter when there is sufficient space.

2. **Merging Traffic**: When merging onto a highway or road, vehicles already on the highway have the right of way. Drivers entering the highway must yield and adjust their speed to merge safely without causing disruption. If there is a designated merge lane, use it to adjust your speed accordingly.

3. **Yielding at Intersections**: At an intersection with no traffic lights or signs, vehicles approaching from the right have the right of way. If two vehicles arrive simultaneously, the vehicle on the right should be allowed to go first. However, drivers should always approach intersections cautiously and be prepared to stop.

4. **Left Turns at Intersections**: When making a left turn at an intersection, drivers must yield to oncoming traffic. Oncoming vehicles have the right of way unless there is a dedicated left turn signal or turn lane. Always ensure the path is clear before completing a left turn.

5. **Pedestrian Crosswalks**: Pedestrians have the right of way at crosswalks, regardless of whether or not there are traffic signals. Drivers must stop to allow pedestrians to cross the street safely, and they should never block a crosswalk while waiting at a light.

6. **School Zones**: When driving through a school zone with children present, drivers must yield to pedestrians and

proceed cautiously, especially during drop-off and pick-up times. Some school zones may have flashing lights indicating when the speed limit is reduced, and it is crucial to obey these limits for safety.

7. **T intersections**: At a T intersection, the vehicle on the through road has the right of way, and the vehicle turning onto the through road must yield. Drivers should always come to a complete stop at a T intersection and look for traffic before proceeding.

8. **Stop Signs**: When approaching an intersection with a stop sign, drivers must come to a complete stop and yield to any oncoming traffic or pedestrians before proceeding. If two vehicles arrive at the same time at a four-way stop, the vehicle on the right has the right of way.

9. **Merge Lanes on Highways**: When entering a highway from an on-ramp, drivers must yield to traffic already on the highway. Vehicles on the highway have the right of way, and drivers entering should adjust their speed to match the flow of traffic before merging safely.

10. **Two-way Stop at Intersections**: If you are driving on a two-way road and approach an intersection with stop signs, you must stop and yield to traffic on the through road. The vehicles traveling on the through road have the right of way.

11. **Traffic Light Situations**: When a traffic light turns green, the vehicles in the intersection should be cleared before proceeding. Drivers must also yield to pedestrians and cyclists in the crosswalk. If turning left at a green light, always yield to oncoming traffic.

12. **Emergency Vehicles**: When an emergency vehicle (such as an ambulance, fire truck, or police car) is approaching with lights and sirens on, drivers must yield the right of way by pulling over to the right side of the road and stopping until the emergency vehicle passes. In certain situations, drivers may need to stop entirely if the emergency vehicle is approaching from the opposite direction.

Understanding who has the right of way in various driving situations helps prevent confusion and reduce the chances of accidents. Drivers must always exercise caution, be aware of their surroundings, and follow traffic laws to keep everyone on the road safe.

QUESTIONNAIRE

1. What is the correct action to take when merging onto a highway?

a) Speed up to match the speed of traffic and enter the highway without stopping.
b) Yield to vehicles already on the highway and adjust your speed to merge safely.
c) Stop at the end of the ramp and wait for a gap in traffic before merging.
d) Accelerate rapidly to ensure you don't hold up traffic on the highway.

Answer: b) Yield to vehicles already on the highway and adjust your speed to merge safely.
Explanation: When merging, vehicles already on the highway

have the right of way. You should adjust your speed to safely merge into the traffic flow without disrupting the flow of traffic.

2. When approaching a roundabout, who has the right of way?

a) Vehicles already inside the roundabout.
b) Vehicles entering the roundabout.
c) Pedestrians.
d) The first vehicle to reach the roundabout.

Answer: a) Vehicles already inside the roundabout.
Explanation: Vehicles already in the roundabout have the right of way. Drivers entering the roundabout must yield and wait for a gap in traffic.

3. What is the correct procedure when approaching a stop sign at an intersection?

a) Slow down and roll through if no other vehicles are present.
b) Come to a complete stop, yield to pedestrians, and then proceed when it is safe.
c) Slow down and proceed without stopping if no other vehicles are visible.
d) Stop only if other vehicles are present.

Answer: b) Come to a complete stop, yield to pedestrians, and then proceed when it is safe.
Explanation: At a stop sign, you are required to come to a full stop, yield to pedestrians, and ensure the intersection is clear before proceeding.

4. Who has the right of way at a four-way stop when two vehicles arrive at the same time?

a) The vehicle on the left.
b) The vehicle on the right.
c) The vehicle turning left.
d) The vehicle with the bigger engine.

Answer: b) The vehicle on the right.
Explanation: At a four-way stop, when two vehicles arrive at the same time, the vehicle on the right has the right of way.

5. What should you do when you approach an intersection with a green light but traffic is blocking the intersection?

a) Proceed with caution, as long as the light is green.
b) Wait behind the line until the intersection is clear.
c) Stop, wait for the next light cycle, and then proceed.
d) Honk your horn and try to move around the blockage.

Answer: b) Wait behind the line until the intersection is clear.
Explanation: If you are unable to clear the intersection, you must wait until the road ahead is clear, even if the light is green.

6. What action should you take when approaching a pedestrian crosswalk with a green light?

a) Continue through the crosswalk if no pedestrians are visible.
b) Stop for pedestrians crossing, even if the light is green.
c) Speed up to pass the crosswalk before pedestrians cross.
d) Wait for the pedestrian signal to change before continuing.

Answer: b) Stop for pedestrians crossing, even if the light is green.
Explanation: Pedestrians have the right of way at crosswalks, and

drivers must stop to allow them to cross safely, regardless of the traffic light.

7. When turning left at an intersection, who has the right of way?

a) The vehicle turning right.
b) Vehicles coming from the opposite direction.
c) Pedestrians crossing the street.
d) The vehicle behind you.

Answer: b) Vehicles coming from the opposite direction.
Explanation: When making a left turn at an intersection, vehicles coming from the opposite direction must be yielded to before completing the turn.

8. What should you do when an emergency vehicle is approaching with sirens and flashing lights?

a) Speed up to get out of the way quickly.
b) Move to the right side of the road and stop.
c) Keep driving at the same speed and avoid changing lanes.
d) Pull over to the left side of the road if you are in the left lane.

Answer: b) Move to the right side of the road and stop.
Explanation: When an emergency vehicle is approaching, you must pull over to the right side of the road and stop to allow the emergency vehicle to pass.

9. At a T intersection, who has the right of way?

a) The vehicle on the through road.
b) The vehicle turning onto the through road.

c) The vehicle that arrives first.
d) The vehicle on the left side.

Answer: a) The vehicle on the through road.
Explanation: At a T intersection, the vehicle on the through road has the right of way, and the vehicle turning onto the through road must yield.

10. If you are stopped at a railroad crossing with a lowered gate, what should you do?

a) Drive around the gate and proceed.
b) Wait for the gate to raise and for the lights to stop flashing.
c) Wait for the train to pass, then proceed immediately.
d) Attempt to cross the tracks if no train is visible.

Answer: b) Wait for the gate to raise and for the lights to stop flashing.
Explanation: Never attempt to drive around a lowered gate. Wait until the gate is raised and the flashing lights stop before crossing the tracks.

Chapter 4

Utah Road Signs

Road signs are an essential part of the road system, helping ensure safety and smooth flow of traffic. In Utah, road signs are categorized into five primary types: regulatory signs, warning signs, informational signs, guide signs, and road markings. Understanding the meanings and proper interpretation of these signs is crucial for all drivers to maintain a safe driving environment.

- **Regulatory Signs**: These signs provide legal instructions or prohibitions. They must be followed by all drivers to ensure the safe and orderly flow of traffic.

- **Warning Signs**: These signs alert drivers to potential hazards or changes in the road ahead, allowing drivers to adjust their behaviour accordingly.

- **Informational Signs**: These signs provide general information, including directions, distances, and other useful facts.

- **Guide Signs**: These signs provide directional guidance for drivers, helping them navigate efficiently.

- **Road Markings**: Painted lines or symbols on the road that convey specific instructions related to lane usage, stopping, or turning.

Regulatory Signs

1. **Speed Limit Sign**

   o **Symbol**: A white rectangle with black numbers

   o **Meaning**: Indicates the maximum or minimum speed at which vehicles can travel on a particular stretch of road.

2. **No Parking**

   o **Symbol**: A white rectangle with red letters or symbols

   o **Meaning**: Indicates areas where parking is not allowed.

3. **Stop Sign**

   o **Symbol**: An octagon with a red background and white letters

   o **Meaning**: Requires vehicles to come to a complete stop at the intersection.

4. **Yield Sign**

   o **Symbol**: An inverted triangle with a red border

   o **Meaning**: Drivers must slow down or stop to yield the right of way to other vehicles or pedestrians.

5. **One Way**

   o **Symbol**: A black arrow on a white background

   o **Meaning**: Indicates that traffic is allowed to flow in only one direction on the road.

6. **Do Not Enter**

   o **Symbol**: A red circle with a white horizontal line across the middle

   o **Meaning**: Marks the entrance of a road where vehicles are prohibited from entering.

7. **No U-Turn**

   o **Symbol**: A black U-shape with a red slash through it

   o **Meaning**: Indicates that making a U-turn at this location is not permitted.

8. **No Left Turn**

   o **Symbol**: A black left arrow with a red slash through it

   o **Meaning**: Prohibits making a left turn at the intersection.

9. **No Right Turn**

   o **Symbol**: A black right arrow with a red slash through it

   o **Meaning**: Prohibits making a right turn at the intersection.

10. **Railroad Crossing**

    o **Symbol**: A white sign with an "X" and black letters "RR"

    o **Meaning**: Alerts drivers to the presence of a railroad crossing ahead.

11. Handicap Parking

- ○ **Symbol**: A blue square with a white wheelchair symbol

- ○ **Meaning**: Designates parking spaces reserved for vehicles with a disabled person's parking permit.

12. School Zone

- ○ **Symbol**: A yellow pentagon with two figures of children crossing

- ○ **Meaning**: Indicates that there is a school nearby and drivers should reduce their speed.

13. Pedestrian Crossing

- ○ **Symbol**: A yellow diamond with a black walking figure

- ○ **Meaning**: Alerts drivers to expect pedestrians crossing the road.

14. Construction Zone

- ○ **Symbol**: An orange diamond with a symbol of a construction worker

- ○ **Meaning**: Indicates an area where road construction or maintenance is taking place.

15. Speed Hump

- ○ **Symbol**: A diamond shape with a picture of a speed hump

- o **Meaning**: Warns drivers of a speed hump or raised area on the road.

16. **No Parking Anytime**

- o **Symbol**: A blue rectangle with a red "P" with a line through it

- o **Meaning**: Indicates that parking is not allowed at any time.

17. **Turn Left or Right Only**

- o **Symbol**: A white rectangle with an arrow pointing left or right

- o **Meaning**: Indicates that drivers must turn left or right, depending on the sign.

18. **Truck Route**

- o **Symbol**: A sign with a truck symbol and an arrow

- o **Meaning**: Indicates that only trucks are permitted to use the specified route.

19. **Lane Use Control**

- o **Symbol**: A sign with an arrow and a red "X"

- o **Meaning**: Indicates that the lane is closed or not available for use.

20. **Parking Meter**

- o **Symbol**: A sign showing a meter with the time limit

- o **Meaning**: Indicates that parking is allowed for a limited time and requires payment.

Warning Signs

1. **Sharp Curve Ahead**

   o **Symbol**: A yellow diamond with a curved arrow

   o **Meaning**: Warns drivers of an upcoming sharp curve.

2. **Slippery When Wet**

   o **Symbol**: A yellow diamond with a car skidding

   o **Meaning**: Warns of a potentially slippery road surface when wet.

3. **Bump Ahead**

   o **Symbol**: A yellow diamond with a bump icon

   o **Meaning**: Indicates a sudden bump or dip in the road.

4. **Deer Crossing**

   o **Symbol**: A yellow diamond with an image of a deer

   o **Meaning**: Alerts drivers that deer may cross the road ahead.

5. **School Crossing**

   o **Symbol**: A yellow diamond with two children walking

   o **Meaning**: Alerts drivers to a school zone with children crossing.

6. **Intersection Ahead**

   o **Symbol**: A yellow diamond with a black cross

   o **Meaning**: Warns of an upcoming intersection.

7. **Side Road**

   o **Symbol**: A yellow diamond with a side road joining the main road

   o **Meaning**: Indicates that a side road intersects with the road you are traveling on.

8. **End of Speed Limit**

   o **Symbol**: A yellow diamond with the number 50 and an arrow

   o **Meaning**: Indicates the end of a specific speed limit zone.

9. **Yield Ahead**

   o **Symbol**: A yellow diamond with a yield symbol

   o **Meaning**: Warns of an upcoming yield sign at the next intersection.

10. **Stop Ahead**

    o **Symbol**: A yellow diamond with a stop sign symbol

    o **Meaning**: Warns of an upcoming stop sign.

11. **Merging Traffic**

    o **Symbol**: A yellow diamond with two arrows merging

o **Meaning**: Indicates that traffic is merging from another lane.

12. Pedestrian Crossing Ahead

o **Symbol**: A yellow diamond with a walking pedestrian symbol

o **Meaning**: Warns drivers of a pedestrian crossing ahead.

13. Road Narrows

o **Symbol**: A yellow diamond with an icon of a narrowing road

o **Meaning**: Indicates that the road narrows ahead.

14. Low Clearance

o **Symbol**: A yellow diamond with a truck under a bridge

o **Meaning**: Warns of a low bridge or overhead obstruction.

15. Loose Gravel

o **Symbol**: A yellow diamond with a picture of gravel

o **Meaning**: Alerts drivers to the presence of loose gravel on the road surface.

16. No Passing Zone

o **Symbol**: A yellow pennant-shaped sign

o **Meaning**: Indicates that passing is not allowed in this area.

17. Road Construction Ahead

- o **Symbol**: A yellow diamond with construction cones

- o **Meaning**: Warns drivers of roadwork ahead.

18. Hill Ahead

- o **Symbol**: A yellow diamond with a steep slope arrow

- o **Meaning**: Indicates a steep hill or incline ahead.

19. Railroad Crossing Ahead

- o **Symbol**: A yellow diamond with a railroad track symbol

- o **Meaning**: Alerts drivers to an upcoming railroad crossing.

20. Falling Rocks

- o **Symbol**: A yellow diamond with falling rock symbols

- o **Meaning**: Warns of a potential hazard from falling rocks along the road.

Informational Signs

Informational signs provide vital information about road conditions, directions, and other helpful data to drivers. They are critical for guiding vehicles safely through roads, particularly when it comes to finding destinations, understanding distances, and staying informed about regulations that may affect driving decisions.

1. **Exit Sign**

     o **Symbol**: A green rectangle with an exit arrow and the word "EXIT"

     o **Meaning**: Indicates the location of an exit off the freeway or major highway.

2. **Distance to Next City**

     o **Symbol**: A green rectangle with the name of a city and the distance

     o **Meaning**: Shows the distance to the next city or major landmark.

3. **Rest Area Ahead**

     o **Symbol**: A blue rectangle with a symbol of a restroom and an arrow

     o **Meaning**: Alerts drivers to an upcoming rest area for stops, typically with facilities such as bathrooms or picnic areas.

4. **Hospital Sign**

     o **Symbol**: A blue square with a white "H" symbol

- o **Meaning**: Indicates the direction to the nearest hospital.

5. **Gas Station Sign**

   - o **Symbol**: A blue square with a fuel pump symbol

   - o **Meaning**: Indicates the location of nearby gas stations along the road.

6. **Food Sign**

   - o **Symbol**: A blue square with a utensil and plate symbol

   - o **Meaning**: Shows the direction to restaurants or dining options.

7. **Lodging Sign**

   - o **Symbol**: A blue square with a bed symbol

   - o **Meaning**: Directs drivers to nearby hotels or accommodations.

8. **Telephone Sign**

   - o **Symbol**: A blue square with a telephone symbol

   - o **Meaning**: Indicates the location of a telephone or public phone booth.

9. **Airport Sign**

   - o **Symbol**: A blue square with an airplane symbol

   - o **Meaning**: Provides directions to the nearest airport.

10. Bike Path Sign

- o **Symbol**: A blue square with a bicycle symbol

- o **Meaning**: Indicates the presence of a bicycle path along the road.

11. Tourist Information Sign

- o **Symbol**: A blue square with an "i" symbol

- o **Meaning**: Directs drivers to the nearest tourist information center.

12. Emergency Detour Route

- o **Symbol**: A yellow diamond with arrows indicating detour direction

- o **Meaning**: Provides alternate routes in case of road closures or emergencies.

13. Truck Route

- o **Symbol**: A rectangular sign with an image of a truck

- o **Meaning**: Marks a designated route for trucks, often to avoid residential areas.

14. No Through Traffic

- o **Symbol**: A white rectangle with a red bar across the middle

- o **Meaning**: Indicates that vehicles cannot pass through a road or area.

15. Scenic Route

o **Symbol**: A green square with a winding road and scenic symbol

o **Meaning**: Directs drivers to a designated scenic route known for its picturesque views.

16. **Speed Advisory**

o **Symbol**: A rectangular sign with speed recommendations

o **Meaning**: Advises a safe or recommended speed for certain road conditions, such as curves or steep slopes.

17. **Toll Road**

o **Symbol**: A green square with a dollar symbol or a toll booth icon

o **Meaning**: Alerts drivers to an upcoming toll road where they must pay a fee for usage.

18. **Weather Conditions Sign**

o **Symbol**: A blue square with a snowflake or other weather-related symbol

o **Meaning**: Provides warnings or information about weather conditions that may affect driving, such as icy roads or rain.

19. **Pedestrian Overpass Sign**

o **Symbol**: A blue square with a pedestrian figure and an overpass symbol o **Meaning**: Indicates the location of a pedestrian overpass or bridge.

20. **Construction Zone Ahead (Info)**

   o **Symbol**: A yellow rectangle with construction cones

   o **Meaning**: Notifies drivers about upcoming construction zones and possible delays, without the direct implication of a hazard.

Guide Signs

Guide signs help with directional guidance and orientation, ensuring that drivers follow the right path towards their destinations. These signs provide important information about route directions, exits, and landmarks.

1. **Exit Information Sign**

   o **Symbol**: A green rectangular sign with exit number and direction

   o **Meaning**: Provides directions and the number of the exit to take for a specific destination or route.

2. **Mile Marker Sign**

   o **Symbol**: A green rectangular sign with mile markers

   o **Meaning**: Displays the current mile marker on highways or roads, useful for navigation or in case of emergencies.

3. **Interstate Route Sign**

   o **Symbol**: A blue and white shield with an interstate number

   o **Meaning**: Identifies the interstate highway and its number, aiding drivers in navigation.

4. **State Route Sign**

   o **Symbol**: A green rectangle with the state route number

   o **Meaning**: Identifies state-specific routes and provides directions for local travel.

5. **Bridge or Tunnel Sign**

   o **Symbol**: A sign with an image of a bridge or tunnel

   o **Meaning**: Indicates the presence of a bridge or tunnel ahead and alerts drivers to the specific conditions associated with them.

6. **Next Exit Sign**

   o **Symbol**: A green sign indicating that the next exit is coming up

   o **Meaning**: Alerts drivers to an upcoming exit that they can take for further travel.

7. **Directional Sign**

   o **Symbol**: A rectangular sign with arrows pointing left, right, or straight ahead o **Meaning**: Helps drivers choose the correct lane or direction to continue on their journey.

8. **Ramp Sign**

   o **Symbol**: A green sign indicating ramp access

   o **Meaning**: Directs drivers to a ramp, either to exit or merge onto another road.

9. **Destination Sign**

   o **Symbol**: A green sign with the name of a city or destination and distance

   o **Meaning**: Informs drivers of the distance to nearby towns, cities, or other landmarks.

10. **HOV Lane Sign**

   o **Symbol**: A green sign with a carpool symbol

   o **Meaning**: Marks lanes designated for high-occupancy vehicles, such as carpool lanes.

11. **Left or Right Turn Only**

   o **Symbol**: A black arrow indicating left or right direction

   o **Meaning**: Indicates that drivers must turn left or right at an intersection, not continue straight.

12. **Dead End**

   o **Symbol**: A sign with a straight line and an arrow showing no further road ahead

- Meaning: Alerts drivers to a dead-end street or road, indicating that there is no through route.

13. **No Outlet**

   - **Symbol**: A sign showing an arrow with a line through it

   - **Meaning**: Indicates a street or road that does not have an exit or outlet.

14. **Road Closed**

   - **Symbol**: A rectangular sign indicating a closed road

   - **Meaning**: Alerts drivers to a road closure, possibly due to construction, accidents, or other reasons.

15. **Detour Sign**

   - **Symbol**: A yellow diamond with arrows indicating a change in direction

   - **Meaning**: Guides drivers to an alternate route around a construction zone or other obstruction.

16. **Exit with Services**

   - **Symbol**: A green sign showing exit directions and service availability, such as gas or food

   - **Meaning**: Points drivers to an exit that provides services such as food, gas, or rest stops.

17. **Intersection Ahead**

   - **Symbol**: A rectangular sign with an image of two intersecting roads

- Meaning: Warns of an intersection ahead, where drivers must slow down and yield as necessary.

18. **Travel Advisory Sign**

- **Symbol**: A sign with a caution symbol and weather-related or traffic condition message

- **Meaning**: Alerts drivers about upcoming hazardous conditions or general travel advisories, such as severe weather or heavy traffic.

19. **No U-Turn Sign**

- **Symbol**: A black U-shaped arrow with a red slash through it

- **Meaning**: Prohibits making a U-turn at this intersection or location.

20. **Lane Ends Sign**

- **Symbol**: A yellow diamond with an arrow and a line indicating a lane reduction

- **Meaning**: Warns drivers of a lane that will end ahead, requiring them to merge into the remaining lanes.

Road Markings

Road markings help control traffic flow, designate lanes, and communicate road conditions. They are typically painted onto the surface of the road and convey important information, such as lane boundaries, turns, or other road instructions.

1. **Solid White Line**

- Symbol: A continuous white line

- Meaning: Indicates that lane changes are prohibited.

2. **Dashed White Line**

   - Symbol: A broken white line

   - Meaning: Allows vehicles to change lanes when safe to do so.

3. **Solid Yellow Line**

   - Symbol: A continuous yellow line

   - Meaning: Indicates that passing is prohibited in both directions.

4. **Dashed Yellow Line**

   - Symbol: A broken yellow line

   - Meaning: Allows passing, but only when it is safe to do so.

5. **Double Solid Yellow Line**

   - Symbol: Two continuous yellow lines

   - Meaning: No passing allowed in either direction.

6. **Centre Turn Lane**

   - Symbol: A lane with dashed yellow lines on both sides and a solid yellow line in the centre

   - Meaning: Indicates a lane reserved for turning vehicles.

7. **Chevron Markings**

   o **Symbol**: V-shaped markings pointing in the direction of the road

   o **Meaning**: Used in sharp curves or hazardous areas to guide drivers and indicate the appropriate path.

8. **Pedestrian Crossing Markings**

   o **Symbol**: White stripes across the road

   o **Meaning**: Indicates a pedestrian crosswalk.

9. **Stop Line**

   o **Symbol**: A solid white line at an intersection

   o **Meaning**: Indicates where vehicles must stop at a stop sign or signal.

10. **Yield Line**

    o **Symbol**: A series of white triangles leading up to a yield sign

    o **Meaning**: Indicates where drivers must yield at an intersection or pedestrian crossing.

11. **Bike Lane Markings**

    o **Symbol**: A bike symbol painted on the road

    o **Meaning**: Designates a lane specifically for bicycles.

12. **HOV Lane Markings**

    o **Symbol**: A diamond symbol in the center of the lane

- o **Meaning**: Identifies lanes reserved for high-occupancy vehicles.

13. **Rumble Strips**

- o **Symbol**: A series of raised, uneven marks on the road

- o **Meaning**: Used to alert drivers when they are veering off the road or nearing a hazard.

14. **Arrow Markings**

- o **Symbol**: Arrows on the road

- o **Meaning**: Indicates the direction of travel or turn lanes.

15. **No Parking Markings**

- o **Symbol**: A solid white line with a "No Parking" symbol

- o **Meaning**: Indicates areas where parking is prohibited.

16. **Crosswalk Markings**

- o **Symbol**: Thick white lines forming a pedestrian crosswalk

- o **Meaning**: Identifies a designated area for pedestrians to cross the road.

17. **Exit Lane Markings**

- o **Symbol**: A solid white line marking the exit lane

- o **Meaning**: Indicates a lane that will take drivers off the main highway or road.

18. Pedestrian Island Markings

- o **Symbol**: A striped area in the center of the crosswalk

- o **Meaning**: Marks a safe area for pedestrians to stop while crossing busy roads.

19. Diamond Lane Markings

- o **Symbol**: Diamond-shaped symbols painted on the road

- o **Meaning**: Marks lanes designated for high-occupancy vehicles or buses.

20. Construction Zone Markings

- o **Symbol**: Cones or barricades painted on the road

- o **Meaning**: Marks areas where road construction or maintenance is in progress.

Knowing the different types of traffic signs and their meanings is crucial to safe and effective driving. Recognizing and understanding these signs allows drivers to make informed decisions and avoid potential hazards. As you continue your journey toward obtaining your Utah driver's license, remember that familiarity with road signs is essential to passing your driving exam and becoming a responsible, confident driver.

| Truck Restrictions Sign | slippery road | No left turn | No right turn | Food | Lodging |

| Fuel Station | Sharp Turn | Construction Zone | Tourism | Bumb Ahead | New city Limit |

| Aiport | distance to city | Directional Arrow | distance sign | Mile marker | Public Transit |

| Turn Only Lane | Bike Route | Arrows | Bike lane | yield line | Camping Site |

| Junction Sign | Trailblazer Sign | Fire Lane Markings | Parking Space | HOV Lane Marking |

REGULATORY SIGNS

Yield   No Turn   One Way   Stop   Do not Enter   Speed Limit   Go   No Parking

WARNING SIGNS

Curve Ahead   Deer Crossing   Railway   School Crossing   Merge   Crosswalks   Curve Ahead

GUIDE SIGNS

    EXIT

Interstate Highway   US highway   Exit   Rest Area   Hospital   Street Sign

ROAD MARKINGS

solid white line   Broken white line   solid Yellow line   Broken Yellow line   double line   crosswalk line   Stop Line

OTHERS

Flagger Ahead   Detour   Uncontrolled Intersections   Narrow Mountain Roads   Roundabout   T-Intersections

QUESTIONNAIRE

1. Which of the following is a regulatory sign that directs a driver to stop, but it is not accompanied by a full stop line?

A) Yield sign
B) Stop sign
C) Speed limit sign
D) Railroad crossing sign

Correct Answer: B) Stop sign
Explanation: A stop sign is a regulatory sign that requires a driver to stop at the intersection. It may not always have a full stop line but still mandates a complete stop.

2. What is the meaning of a yellow diamond-shaped sign with a symbol of a truck going down a hill?

A) Truck parking ahead
B) Warning of steep incline for trucks
C) Truck weight limit
D) Truck exit ahead

Correct Answer: B) Warning of steep incline for trucks
Explanation: The yellow diamond-shaped sign with a truck going downhill indicates that the road has a steep incline, which may require trucks to take extra caution.

3. What does a rectangular white sign with black text "RIGHT LANE MUST TURN RIGHT" indicate?

A) Right lane is a dedicated right turn lane
B) Right lane can only turn left

C) Drivers in the right lane must stop at the next light
D) Right lane must yield to traffic

Correct Answer: A) Right lane is a dedicated right turn lane
Explanation: This regulatory sign means that vehicles in the right lane are required to turn right at the upcoming intersection.

4. What is the significance of a circular red and white sign with a black "X" and two R symbols?

A) Stop sign
B) Railroad crossing
C) School crossing
D) Yield sign

Correct Answer: B) Railroad crossing
Explanation: A circular red and white sign with a black "X" and two "R" symbols is a railroad crossing sign. It warns drivers to stop or slow down as they approach a railway crossing.

5. When approaching a yellow diamond-shaped sign with an icon of a person walking, what should you do?

A) Speed up to pass the pedestrian area quickly
B) Stop and yield to pedestrians in the crosswalk
C) Continue driving at the same speed without stopping
D) Look for the nearest crosswalk to turn

Correct Answer: B) Stop and yield to pedestrians in the crosswalk
Explanation: This sign indicates a pedestrian crossing. Drivers must slow down and be prepared to yield to pedestrians who may be crossing the road.

6. Which of the following road signs indicates that there is a temporary road obstruction in the path of travel?

A) Construction zone sign
B) No parking sign
C) Lane merge sign
D) Winding road sign

Correct Answer: A) Construction zone sign
Explanation: A construction zone sign indicates that there is roadwork or an obstruction ahead, and drivers should reduce speed and be aware of workers or equipment.

7. What does a blue square sign with a white "P" and a crossed circle symbol indicate?

A) Parking allowed
B) No parking at any time
C) Parking for disabled only
D) Public parking ahead

Correct Answer: B) No parking at any time
Explanation: This sign is a no parking symbol, indicating that parking is not allowed in that area at any time, regardless of circumstances.

8. What does a brown rectangular sign with a white symbol of a bed represent?

A) Hotel or lodging available nearby
B) Roadside rest area
C) Upcoming hospital
D) Restroom facilities ahead

Correct Answer: A) Hotel or lodging available nearby
Explanation: A brown rectangular sign with a bed symbol indicates that there is a hotel or lodging nearby for travellers needing accommodation.

9. What should you do when you see a yellow diamond-shaped sign with a truck symbol and a downward pointing arrow?

A) Prepare to slow down for an upcoming steep incline
B) Stop and wait for a traffic signal
C) Continue driving at normal speed without slowing down
D) Prepare to stop for a train crossing

Correct Answer: A) Prepare to slow down for an upcoming steep incline
Explanation: This sign indicates that there is a steep grade ahead, specifically a downhill slope for trucks. Drivers should slow down to maintain control of their vehicle.

10. What is the meaning of a rectangular white sign with black diagonal stripes, indicating a lane ahead?

A) Lane for emergency vehicles only
B) Lane ends ahead
C) Lane reserved for buses only
D) Lane closed for construction

Correct Answer: B) Lane ends ahead
Explanation: This white sign with black diagonal stripes indicates that the lane will end shortly, and drivers should be prepared to merge into another lane.

Chapter 5

Best Driving Practices

In Utah, as in any other state, adhering to best driving practices not only ensures the safety of yourself but also that of other road users. The state's diverse terrain and weather conditions necessitate careful attention to driving habits. Utah's traffic laws are designed to promote safe driving, reduce accidents, and create a cooperative environment on the road.

First, always stay aware of your surroundings. The ability to anticipate potential hazards—such as vehicles merging, pedestrians crossing, or wildlife on the road—is crucial. Defensive driving is a key component of this practice, where you take actions to avoid accidents even when the other driver is at fault. Second, always obey speed limits and be mindful of changing traffic conditions. Driving too fast for road conditions, especially in areas with heavy snow or rain, can result in loss of vehicle control. Third, make use of the road signs and markings. They serve to guide you, warn you, and help you navigate roads safely. Fourth, driving with courtesy, such as yielding the right of way when appropriate, allowing safe merging, and maintaining a calm demeanour behind the wheel, fosters a more peaceful road environment. Additionally, Utah's mountain roads, with their steep inclines and sharp turns, require specialized driving techniques, such as downshifting in manual vehicles to reduce speed on descents. Finally, driving with patience and caution through Utah's popular tourist areas, where traffic can be heavy, will not only make your journey more pleasant but also safe.

Defensive Driving Techniques

Defensive driving is a proactive approach to road safety. It goes beyond basic driving skills and focuses on anticipating potential hazards and avoiding them through cautious and deliberate driving practices. Here are several critical techniques used in defensive driving:

1. **Stay Alert and Avoid Distractions**: Always keep your eyes on the road and hands on the wheel. Distractions such as texting, talking on the phone, or adjusting the radio can divert your attention from the road, increasing the risk of accidents. Even a brief lapse in concentration can be dangerous.

2. **Maintain a Safe Following Distance**: One of the most fundamental principles of defensive driving is to ensure there is enough space between your car and the vehicle in front of you. This gives you more time to react to sudden stops, changes in speed, or unexpected obstacles. The "three-second rule" is commonly used, where you should maintain a distance that allows you to count three seconds between your car and the one ahead of you.

3. **Be Prepared for the Unexpected**: Always anticipate what other drivers might do, even if they are not following the rules of the road. This means being ready to react quickly in case another driver suddenly changes lanes without signalling, runs a red light, or cuts you off.

4. **Use Your Mirrors Frequently**: Constantly check your rear-view and side mirrors to stay aware of traffic conditions behind you. This helps you to avoid surprises and provides

an opportunity to adjust your driving accordingly. You should check your mirrors every 5 to 8 seconds.

5. **Be Cautious at Intersections**: Intersections are among the most dangerous places on the road, as they involve interactions between multiple vehicles. Before entering an intersection, always look both ways, even if you have a green light. Be prepared to stop for red-light runners or pedestrians who may be crossing unexpectedly.

6. **Control Your Speed**: Always adjust your speed to match the road conditions. If the road is wet, foggy, or icy, reduce your speed to maintain control of your vehicle. Speeding reduces your reaction time and increases the severity of potential accidents.

7. **Use Your Signals**: Always signal before changing lanes or making turns. Signalling alerts other drivers of your intentions, allowing them to adjust their speed or position accordingly.

8. **Avoid Blind Spots**: Every vehicle has blind spots, areas around the car where other vehicles may be hidden from view. Always check your blind spots before changing lanes or merging.

9. **Know Your Vehicle**: Understanding how your vehicle performs in different conditions, whether on a wet road or during heavy braking, helps you to drive defensively. Regular maintenance, such as tire pressure checks and brake inspections, also enhances your safety.

Safe Following Distances

Maintaining a safe following distance is one of the most critical driving habits to ensure road safety. The distance between your car and the vehicle ahead of you determines how much time you have to react if the vehicle suddenly stops or changes speed. Without an adequate gap, you might not have enough time to avoid a collision.

A safe following distance gives you a "buffer zone" to assess the road ahead and respond to hazards. The general rule is to maintain at least a 3-second gap from the vehicle in front of you. This means when the car ahead of you passes a stationary object, such as a road sign or a tree, you should be able to count at least three seconds before you pass the same object. In ideal weather and traffic conditions, a 3-second gap is typically sufficient. However, this distance should be increased in the following situations:

- **Adverse weather conditions**: Rain, fog, snow, or ice can reduce traction and increase stopping distance. In such conditions, a 5 to 6-second following distance is recommended.

- **Heavy traffic**: In congested conditions, it is easy for vehicles to stop suddenly. Maintaining a larger gap will help you avoid rear-end collisions.

- **Driving behind large vehicles**: Trucks and buses block your view of the road ahead. Allowing extra distance enables you to see further down the road and react to potential hazards.

- **Night driving**: In low-light conditions, your ability to see obstacles and react quickly is limited. Increasing your following distance to 4 or 5 seconds at night provides more time to identify potential issues.

- **Towing a trailer**: If you are towing a trailer, your stopping distance increases. A 5-second or longer gap is advisable to ensure you can stop safely.

- **Rural roads**: On roads without a central lane or on winding, narrow roads, increasing the following distance ensures there is room to manoeuvre or stop when necessary.

In addition to adjusting your following distance, it is essential to remain aware of your surroundings and always be prepared to stop or slow down at a moment's notice. Practicing patience and remaining calm while driving will help you maintain a safe and reasonable gap from other vehicles.

Proper Use of Headlights

Headlights are crucial for safe driving, especially at night, in low visibility, or during adverse weather conditions. Understanding when and how to use your headlights can significantly improve your safety and the safety of other road users.

When to Use Headlights:

- **Night Driving**: Headlights should always be used when driving between dusk and dawn. Even if the streets are lit, headlights are necessary to improve your visibility of the road, pedestrians, and other vehicles.

- **Fog**: In foggy conditions, low beams should be used to reduce glare. High beams can reflect off the fog and make visibility worse.

- **Rain and Snow**: During heavy rain or snow, use your headlights to make your vehicle more visible to other drivers. Using high beams in rain can cause glare and should be avoided.

- **Slippery Roads**: Even during the day, headlights should be turned on when driving on slippery or icy roads to alert other drivers to your presence.

- **Merging or Changing Lanes**: Turn on your headlights when changing lanes or merging, especially in low-light conditions, to improve visibility for other drivers.

- **Entering Tunnels**: Many tunnels have reduced light levels. Use headlights as soon as you approach the tunnel entrance to ensure better visibility.

How to Use Headlights Properly:

- **Low Beams**: Low beams should be used in most situations where there is adequate street lighting or when driving behind another vehicle. They allow you to see the road ahead without blinding other drivers.

- **High Beams**: High beams are ideal for driving on dark, unlit roads with no oncoming traffic. Use them to see farther down the road. However, always dim your high beams when approaching other vehicles or when following closely behind another vehicle.

- **Daytime Running Lights**: Many modern vehicles are equipped with daytime running lights, which increase visibility during the day. However, these lights do not function as headlights and do not illuminate the road in low visibility conditions, so they should not replace the use of headlights at night.

- **Fog Lights**: Fog lights are designed to illuminate the road directly in front of the vehicle when driving in fog, rain, or snow. They are typically mounted lower on the car and should be used in conjunction with low beams. Avoid using fog lights when there is no fog, as they can cause unnecessary glare for other drivers.

- **Headlight Alignment**: Ensure that your headlights are properly aligned. Misaligned headlights can create blind spots for other drivers or fail to adequately illuminate the road in front of you. Regular checks and adjustments are important for safety.

Common Mistakes to Avoid:

- **Using high beams in fog**: High beams should never be used in fog, rain, or snow because the light reflects off the moisture in the air, causing glare and reducing visibility.

- **Driving without headlights at dawn or dusk**: Even when there is a faint amount of light, it is still important to use headlights to ensure your vehicle is visible to others.

- **Not dimming high beams**: Failing to dim your high beams when approaching oncoming traffic can blind other drivers, leading to accidents.

Navigating in Adverse Weather Conditions

Adverse weather conditions such as rain, snow, fog, ice, and strong winds significantly affect driving safety. Understanding how to navigate these conditions safely is crucial for reducing the risk of accidents.

Rain:

When driving in rain, reduce your speed and increase your following distance. Water on the road can create slippery conditions, making it harder for tires to grip the pavement. Hydroplaning, where your tires lose contact with the road, can occur at speeds as low as 35 mph in heavy rain. To prevent hydroplaning, slow down, avoid abrupt steering, and ensure your tires are in good condition with proper tread depth.

Snow and Ice:

Snow and ice present some of the most hazardous driving conditions. When driving in snow, it is essential to drive slowly and keep a greater distance from the vehicle ahead. Braking should be done gently to avoid skidding. In icy conditions, avoid sudden movements, and drive in the tracks left by other vehicles to reduce the risk of slipping. If you encounter black ice, which is particularly dangerous because it is hard to see, avoid making sharp turns or braking suddenly.

Fog:

In foggy conditions, visibility is severely reduced. Always use low-beam headlights, as high beams will reflect off the fog and make it more difficult to see. Reduce your speed and increase your following distance. If visibility is so poor that you can't see more than a few feet ahead, pull over to the side of the road and wait for the fog to lift.

Strong Winds:

Strong winds can make it difficult to control your vehicle, especially if you're driving a larger vehicle such as an SUV or truck. Keep both hands on the wheel and remain calm. Avoid passing large vehicles in windy conditions, as they can create turbulence that makes it harder to maintain control of your vehicle.

Driving Through Flooded Areas:

Avoid driving through flooded areas whenever possible. Water can quickly disable your vehicle, and it is difficult to assess how deep the water is. If you must drive through a flooded area, move slowly and ensure that your vehicle is not submerged in water.

General Tips for Adverse Weather:

- **Check the weather before you drive**: Knowing the conditions ahead of time can help you prepare for potential challenges.

- **Use proper tires**: Winter tires provide better traction on snow and ice, while all-season tires are suitable for milder conditions.

- **Ensure good visibility**: Keep your windows clean, your defroster on, and your windshield wipers in good condition to ensure you can see clearly in poor weather.

Avoiding Road Rage

Road rage is a common issue that can escalate quickly, often leading to dangerous and aggressive driving. However, avoiding road rage requires patience, self-control, and an understanding of how to handle frustrating situations calmly.

To begin with, it's important to recognize the triggers that can lead to road rage. These can include being cut off by another driver, slow drivers in the fast lane, or getting stuck in heavy traffic. However, rather than reacting impulsively, it's crucial to remain calm. Taking deep breaths and counting to ten can help calm your emotions. Avoid engaging in aggressive behaviours such as tailgating or attempting to "teach someone a lesson" by speeding or making sudden lane changes.

Additionally, it's vital to realize that we cannot control the actions of others. Getting upset or angry will not change the behaviour of other drivers but could escalate the situation. Instead, focus on controlling your own actions and remaining composed behind the wheel. If another driver is tailgating you or driving aggressively, avoid making eye contact or responding with gestures. Simply move to a different lane if possible and let them pass.

In situations where you feel that someone's driving is putting you in danger, prioritize safety. If necessary, pull over and let the other vehicle pass to avoid confrontation. Never engage in road rage behaviour, such as aggressive honking or chasing another vehicle, as this can lead to severe accidents.

If you do encounter someone who is engaging in road rage, it is best to avoid retaliating. Maintain a safe distance and, if necessary, report the aggressive driver to the authorities. Always prioritize your safety and avoid escalating conflicts on the road.

Lastly, it's important to manage your own stress levels. If you feel that the pressure of your day is affecting your driving, consider taking a few moments to relax and clear your mind before getting on the road. Reducing stress can significantly decrease the chances of reacting aggressively when faced with frustrating situations.

Navigating Tourist Areas

Navigating through areas with heavy tourist traffic requires special attention and patience. In tourist-heavy locations, such as national parks, historical landmarks, or popular city centres, traffic congestion and unfamiliar road layouts are common. Understanding how to drive safely and effectively in these areas will enhance your experience while keeping you and others safe on the road.

First, always be aware that tourists may be unfamiliar with local road systems, often resulting in erratic or unpredictable driving behaviour. Keep a safe distance from vehicles and be patient with slower drivers. They may be looking for parking or taking time to read road signs, so give them space to manoeuvre.

Second, parking can become a challenge in tourist areas. Look for designated parking lots or garages rather than trying to find parking on the street, especially during peak tourist seasons. If you must park on the street, be mindful of any parking restrictions or time limits to avoid fines or towing.

Third, watch for pedestrians, cyclists, and tourists who may be distracted while exploring. Tourist areas often have crosswalks and pedestrian zones where people may step out into the road without warning. Slow down, give pedestrians the right of way, and always watch for cyclists, as they may be sharing the road.

Navigating narrow streets or unfamiliar intersections in tourist zones may require additional caution. Be aware of one-way streets, particularly in older cities or areas with historic districts, where road signs may be in short supply. If you're unsure of the directions, use a GPS or ask for help to avoid confusion.

Lastly, during peak seasons, tourist areas may experience heavier traffic, making patience essential. Plan your trips during off-peak hours if possible to avoid getting stuck in congestion. If traffic jams occur, stay calm and maintain a safe following distance. Always remember that patience and courtesy go a long way in ensuring safe travels in busy tourist areas.

Hurricane Preparedness for Drivers

Driving during hurricane season requires increased vigilance and preparation due to the hazardous conditions that can arise from storms, such as flooding, strong winds, and poor visibility. One of the first steps in preparing for driving during a hurricane is ensuring that your vehicle is in optimal working condition. This includes checking tire pressure, fluid levels, and the functionality of windshield wipers and headlights, all of which are critical during adverse weather conditions.

When planning travel during hurricane season, it's important to monitor weather forecasts and stay informed about any approaching storms. If possible, avoid traveling during a hurricane warning. Strong winds can cause tree branches, debris, or power lines to fall, creating serious risks for drivers. If you must drive, reduce your speed to maintain control of your vehicle on wet, slippery roads. Also, keep a greater following distance to allow ample time to react to unexpected conditions.

In the event that you find yourself driving during a heavy downpour or flood-prone areas, avoid driving through standing water. Just a few inches of water can cause your vehicle to lose traction and stall. If you encounter a flooded road, turn around and find an alternate route. Keep your vehicle's headlights on to increase visibility, and use your windshield wipers at the highest setting to ensure maximum clarity. Lastly, carry an emergency kit with essentials like bottled water, snacks, a flashlight, a first-aid kit, and a charged phone to stay prepared in case of unexpected delays.

Eco-Friendly Driving Practices

Driving in an eco-friendly manner can significantly reduce your environmental impact while also conserving fuel and saving money. Several techniques can be employed to achieve this, and they not only benefit the environment but also help improve the longevity and efficiency of your vehicle.

First, one of the most effective ways to drive efficiently is by reducing your speed. Driving at speeds over 50 mph can increase fuel consumption due to the higher air resistance encountered at faster speeds. Maintaining a steady speed on highways or long stretches of road without frequent accelerations and decelerations can significantly reduce fuel use. Using cruise control on highways is also helpful, as it prevents unnecessary speed fluctuations, which tend to increase fuel consumption.

Smooth driving habits are another critical factor in improving fuel efficiency. Avoid sudden starts and stops, as rapid acceleration and braking waste fuel. Instead, try to anticipate traffic flow and decelerate gradually when approaching stops or red lights. This helps reduce fuel usage and prevents unnecessary strain on the engine and braking system.

Proper tire maintenance is essential in eco-friendly driving. Tires that are under-inflated can reduce fuel efficiency by increasing rolling resistance, which requires the engine to work harder to maintain speed. Check tire pressure regularly and ensure it matches the manufacturer's recommendation, which can typically be found in the owner's manual or on the inside of the driver's side door. In addition, rotating your tires regularly can help ensure even wear and prolong their life, further reducing your environmental footprint.

Another crucial aspect of eco-friendly driving is vehicle maintenance. Keeping your engine tuned and replacing air filters as needed ensures that your car is running efficiently, consuming less fuel and emitting fewer pollutants. Regular oil changes are also important for maintaining engine health and improving fuel economy. A well-maintained vehicle operates more smoothly, reduces exhaust emissions, and optimizes fuel consumption.

Driving in the right gear is also important for reducing fuel consumption, particularly in manual transmission vehicles. Shift to higher gears as soon as possible to minimize engine strain and fuel waste. Also, avoid driving with unnecessary weight in your vehicle, such as heavy items in the trunk, as this can reduce fuel efficiency.

Finally, eco-friendly driving practices extend to your choice of vehicle. If possible, consider purchasing a hybrid or electric vehicle, which use less fuel and produce fewer emissions than traditional gasoline-powered cars. If buying a new vehicle isn't feasible, opt for one with better fuel efficiency ratings. Taking public transportation, carpooling, or using alternative modes of transport, such as biking or walking, are also great ways to reduce your carbon footprint.

Vehicle Maintenance and Safety Checks

Regular vehicle maintenance and safety checks are essential to ensure that your car remains roadworthy, safe, and efficient. Neglecting these practices can lead to mechanical breakdowns, costly repairs, and, most importantly, compromised safety on the road.

Before embarking on any trip, it is vital to conduct a pre-trip inspection of your vehicle. Begin by checking the condition of your tires. Ensure that they are properly inflated to the recommended levels and check for any signs of wear, such as cracks or bald spots. Tires in good condition help improve fuel efficiency and handling, reducing the risk of accidents caused by skidding or tire blowouts. Rotate your tires regularly to promote even wear and extend their lifespan.

Next, inspect your vehicle's oil and fluid levels. Oil plays a crucial role in lubricating your engine and preventing it from overheating. Regular oil changes, as recommended by the manufacturer, ensure that the engine operates smoothly. Check the coolant, brake fluid, transmission fluid, and windshield washer fluid levels. Top them up as needed, and if any of these fluids appear dirty or low, schedule a maintenance appointment to address potential issues.

The brakes are another critical safety component of your vehicle. Ensure that the brake pads are in good condition and the braking system functions properly. If you hear any unusual noises when braking, such as squealing or grinding, it could indicate worn brake pads or other brake system issues. Immediate attention is required to avoid potential brake failure.

Another area to inspect is your vehicle's lights and signals. Check that all headlights, taillights, brake lights, and turn signals are functioning properly. Malfunctioning lights can impair visibility, making it difficult for other drivers to see your vehicle, especially in low-light conditions. Also, check that your horn, wipers, and washers are working to ensure that you can alert others in case of an emergency and maintain a clear view of the road in adverse weather conditions.

Ensure that your vehicle's battery is in good working condition. A weak or old battery can lead to unexpected breakdowns. If your vehicle is showing signs of starting trouble or the battery is over three years old, have it tested and replaced if necessary. An unreliable battery can leave you stranded and unable to start your vehicle when you need it most.

Lastly, regularly replace air filters to ensure that the engine receives sufficient airflow. Clogged air filters can lead to decreased engine performance, lower fuel efficiency, and increased emissions. Clean filters also help extend the life of your vehicle's engine.

Scheduling regular maintenance checks with a certified mechanic is essential for keeping your car in optimal condition. Following the manufacturer's recommended maintenance schedule ensures that your vehicle continues to run smoothly and reduces the risk of expensive repairs down the road. Pre-trip inspections, regular maintenance, and addressing potential issues early are critical to maintaining roadworthiness and ensuring your safety and the safety of others on the road.

Handling Emergencies

Handling emergencies while driving is an essential skill that can make all the difference in ensuring your safety and the safety of others. Whether you are facing a vehicle breakdown, an accident, or a medical emergency, knowing the proper steps to take can help you manage the situation calmly and effectively.

In the event of a vehicle breakdown, the first step is to remain calm and pull over to a safe location. If you are on the highway or a busy road, try to steer your car onto the shoulder or an off-ramp to avoid blocking traffic. Once your vehicle is safely out of the way, turn on your hazard lights to alert other drivers of your situation. If your vehicle is still running but unsafe to drive, it is important to turn it off to prevent further damage or risk. If you have a roadside assistance service, contact them for help, providing them with your exact location.

If you are involved in an accident, it is essential to assess the situation immediately. First, check yourself and any passengers for injuries. If anyone is injured, call emergency services right away and provide them with clear details of the situation. Do not attempt to move any injured individuals unless there is an immediate risk, such as fire. If the accident is minor and there are no injuries, move your vehicle to a safe spot to avoid further collisions. Exchange insurance and contact details with the other driver(s), but avoid admitting fault at the scene. Document the incident by taking photos and writing down the details of the accident.

For medical emergencies, such as a heart attack or seizure while driving, the priority is to safely stop the vehicle and get assistance. If you feel unwell or experience symptoms of an emergency, pull over to the side of the road. Turn on your hazard lights to signal distress and attempt to contact emergency services or a family member for help. If possible, direct the vehicle to a safe location where help can easily reach you. If you are unable to drive, leave the car in a secure location and wait for assistance.

Regardless of the emergency, your safety is paramount. When dealing with any roadside emergency, always remain calm and assess the situation before taking action. If necessary, seek help from professionals or emergency services. In some situations, knowing the basic steps to take in handling a breakdown or accident can prevent further harm and allow for timely and efficient assistance. Always be prepared and have an emergency kit in your vehicle, as this can provide critical tools and supplies in an emergency situation.

QUESTIONNAIRE

1. When driving during hurricane season, what is the first action a driver should take to ensure their safety?

A) Drive at the highest speed possible to reach a safe area quickly.

B) Monitor weather forecasts and avoid traveling if a hurricane is expected.

C) Turn off headlights and drive cautiously through flooded areas.

D) Wait for emergency personnel to clear the roads before proceeding.

Correct Answer: B) Monitor weather forecasts and avoid traveling if a hurricane is expected.

Explanation: The best course of action is to avoid traveling if there is a hurricane warning. It's important to stay informed and take preventive measures to avoid the dangers associated with strong winds and flooding.

2. What is the primary environmental benefit of maintaining proper tire pressure in your vehicle?

A) Reduces tire wear and extends their life.

B) Reduces fuel efficiency by increasing rolling resistance.

C) Enhances the vehicle's air conditioning system.

D) Increases fuel consumption by causing the vehicle to consume more power.

Correct Answer: A) Reduces tire wear and extends their life.

Explanation: Proper tire pressure helps distribute the weight of the vehicle evenly across the tires, which reduces premature wear and increases fuel efficiency, contributing to the reduction of overall environmental impact.

3. What is the most effective driving technique to improve fuel efficiency when driving on highways?

A) Rapid acceleration and frequent braking.

B) Maintaining a steady speed and using cruise control.

C) Driving at maximum speed to minimize travel time.

D) Shifting to lower gears frequently.

Correct Answer: B) Maintaining a steady speed and using cruise control.

Explanation: Maintaining a steady speed and using cruise control reduces fuel consumption by eliminating unnecessary fluctuations in speed, which can waste fuel.

4. Which of the following best describes a "pre-trip inspection" for a vehicle?

A) Checking the exterior lights only.

B) Inspecting tires, fluids, brakes, and lights before driving.

C) Cleaning the interior of the vehicle.

D) Performing engine diagnostics with a mobile app.

Correct Answer: B) Inspecting tires, fluids, brakes, and lights before driving.

Explanation: A thorough pre-trip inspection involves checking critical components like tires, fluids, brakes, and lights to ensure the vehicle is in optimal condition before hitting the road.

5. What is the significance of keeping your vehicle's engine tuned?

A) It maximizes the number of passengers the vehicle can carry.

B) It improves the vehicle's fuel efficiency and reduces emissions.

C) It enhances the vehicle's speed and acceleration.

D) It extends the life of the vehicle's air conditioning system.

Correct Answer: B) It improves the vehicle's fuel efficiency and reduces emissions.

Explanation: Regular engine tuning ensures that the engine runs smoothly, improving fuel efficiency and reducing harmful emissions, which benefits both the vehicle and the environment.

6. What action should you take if your vehicle begins to overheat while driving?

A) Continue driving until you reach the next service station.

B) Turn off the engine immediately and pull over to a safe location.

C) Turn on the air conditioning to cool the engine down.

D) Accelerate to increase airflow and cool the engine.

Correct Answer: B) Turn off the engine immediately and pull over to a safe location.

Explanation: Continuing to drive with an overheating engine can cause severe damage. Turning off the engine and pulling over allows the vehicle to cool safely and prevents engine failure.

7. Which of the following actions is NOT recommended during an emergency roadside situation?

A) Turning on your hazard lights.

B) Moving your vehicle to a secure, safe area.

C) Exiting the vehicle and standing by the roadside.

D) Calling for roadside assistance or emergency services.

Correct Answer: C) Exiting the vehicle and standing by the roadside.

Explanation: Exiting the vehicle and standing near traffic places you at risk. It's safer to remain inside the vehicle until help arrives or until the situation is under control.

8. When approaching a medical emergency while driving, the priority is to:

A) Continue driving to your destination while seeking medical attention.

B) Pull over to a safe area and call emergency services.

C) Attempt to diagnose and treat the condition yourself.

D) Ignore the situation and keep driving until it resolves.

Correct Answer: B) Pull over to a safe area and call emergency services.

Explanation: The priority during a medical emergency is to safely pull over, stop driving, and call emergency services immediately. This ensures that help can reach you without putting anyone at further risk.

9. What is the role of hazard lights when your vehicle is involved in a breakdown?

A) They alert other drivers that your vehicle is in motion.

B) They signal to other drivers that you are ready to continue driving.

C) They inform other drivers of a potential hazard or emergency situation.

D) They are used to indicate a malfunction with your engine.

Correct Answer: C) They inform other drivers of a potential hazard or emergency situation.

Explanation: Hazard lights are used to alert other drivers to the presence of a stationary or disabled vehicle, which helps prevent accidents by making your vehicle more visible.

10. How can driving at high speeds in adverse weather conditions affect your vehicle's performance?

A) It improves fuel efficiency and reduces emissions.

B) It enhances tire traction and braking response.

C) It increases the risk of hydroplaning and reduces stopping distance.

D) It stabilizes the vehicle and reduces the effects of weather hazards.

Correct Answer: C) It increases the risk of hydroplaning and reduces stopping distance.

Explanation: Driving at high speeds during adverse weather, such as rain or snow, reduces the traction of your tires and can increase the likelihood of hydroplaning, making it harder to stop or control your vehicle.

Chapter 6

Defensive Driving in Utah

Defensive driving is a vital concept for all drivers, but it holds special significance in Utah, where a range of weather conditions, challenging terrain, and dense urban traffic can present unique risks on the road. Defensive driving involves anticipating potential hazards and reacting proactively to avoid accidents. In Utah, defensive driving is encouraged by the Department of Motor Vehicles (DMV) and is integrated into the state's laws and driver education programs.

The state's traffic environment can include everything from mountainous roads, which require careful manoeuvring, to fast-paced freeway traffic in cities like Salt Lake City. Defensive driving aims to reduce risk and improve driver awareness through continuous scanning of the road, an understanding of traffic laws, and applying safe driving practices at all times. This includes maintaining appropriate following distances, using mirrors effectively, signalling in advance, and avoiding aggressive driving behaviours such as tailgating or speeding. Moreover, driving defensively means staying calm and patient in situations where other drivers may act unpredictably or recklessly.

Defensive driving courses are available for drivers seeking to reduce points on their driving record or improve their driving skills. In Utah, taking a defensive driving course may be required by the court following certain traffic violations, and it can also reduce insurance premiums for eligible drivers. Utah's focus on defensive driving helps ensure that drivers are well-equipped to handle the challenges of the road safely and responsibly.

The Importance of Defensive Driving

Defensive driving is not simply a set of guidelines to follow; it is a mindset that prioritizes safety, awareness, and precaution at all times while behind the wheel. It's crucial because the road environment is unpredictable, and even the most experienced drivers can find themselves in dangerous situations caused by factors beyond their control. From erratic drivers to unexpected weather conditions, defensive driving ensures that a driver can avoid accidents or mitigate their severity.

One of the primary reasons defensive driving is so important is because it reduces the likelihood of collisions, particularly in situations where other drivers may not be as cautious. Even if a driver is following all of the proper rules and regulations, they can still find themselves at risk due to the actions of others on the road. Defensive driving prepares a driver to anticipate potential dangers such as abrupt stops, unpredictable lane changes, or impaired drivers. By constantly scanning the environment and staying alert, a defensive driver can react swiftly to avoid dangerous situations.

Beyond the obvious benefit of preventing accidents, defensive driving also helps reduce the severity of accidents when they do occur. For instance, maintaining a safe following distance can give a driver enough time to react to sudden stops or changes in traffic flow. This additional buffer can prevent rear-end collisions and minimize the impact of unavoidable accidents. Moreover, defensive drivers are better equipped to handle dangerous weather conditions, such as rain, snow, or fog. By adjusting their speed, using headlights properly, and maintaining distance, they are more likely to retain control of the vehicle during adverse conditions.

Additionally, defensive driving promotes good judgment and patience, which are crucial for staying calm in stressful driving situations. It encourages drivers to avoid aggressive behaviors like speeding, tailgating, and road rage, which can escalate situations unnecessarily. Defensive drivers tend to make more thoughtful decisions, such as yielding to other drivers when necessary, and they prioritize the safety of themselves and others on the road. This approach is essential for not only protecting oneself but also for fostering a safer driving environment for everyone.

In a broader sense, defensive driving also contributes to safer roads for pedestrians, cyclists, and other vulnerable road users. By being aware of one's surroundings and anticipating possible hazards, defensive drivers help avoid situations that could harm others on the road. As a result, defensive driving is a key component of reducing traffic fatalities and injuries, which is particularly important in Utah, where rural roads and high-speed highways pose additional risks.

Finally, defensive driving helps mitigate the financial consequences of accidents. Accidents, even minor ones, can result in costly repairs, increased insurance premiums, and potential legal liabilities. By reducing the likelihood of an accident, defensive driving not only protects the driver but also reduces the financial burden of collisions. As traffic laws become stricter and insurance premiums rise, defensive driving becomes even more valuable for both personal safety and financial wellbeing.

Identifying and Avoiding Hazards

Hazard identification is a critical skill for every defensive driver, as it allows them to anticipate and avoid potential dangers before they escalate into accidents. Hazards can come in many forms, including environmental factors, other drivers' behaviour, and road conditions. A defensive driver's ability to recognize and respond to these hazards is essential for maintaining safety on the road.

To start, it's important to constantly scan the road and be aware of what is happening around you. Keep an eye on the behaviour of other drivers, as well as any changes in road conditions. For example, if a car suddenly changes lanes without signalling or cuts you off, it's crucial to be prepared to react appropriately. This might mean slowing down, moving to a safer position, or even preparing to stop if necessary. By anticipating these actions, defensive drivers can avoid collisions and mitigate the impact of unexpected manoeuvres by other drivers.

Weather conditions also present significant hazards that require heightened attention. Rain, fog, snow, and icy roads can make driving much more dangerous, especially if you're not prepared. A defensive driver should adjust their speed to match weather conditions, allowing for extra stopping distance and slower cornering. Additionally, using headlights appropriately in low visibility conditions can help other drivers see you and reduce the risk of accidents.

Another common hazard is poor road conditions. Potholes, uneven surfaces, and construction zones can catch a driver off guard if they are not paying attention. Defensive drivers should always be alert for road signs indicating upcoming changes, such as detours or roadwork. If the road surface is poor, slowing down and increasing following distance can help prevent accidents. Keeping your eyes on the road ahead, especially in unfamiliar or challenging areas, allows you to identify potential hazards early and avoid them.

Distracted drivers are another major hazard, as they can often act unpredictably. Defensive driving requires constant awareness of other vehicles and a preparedness to react to erratic driving behaviour. Whether a driver is texting, using a phone, or otherwise distracted, defensive drivers should maintain a safe distance and be ready to take evasive action if necessary. By maintaining a position that gives you plenty of time to react, you can reduce the risk of an accident caused by another driver's distraction.

Finally, it is essential to recognize the hazards presented by driving at night. Reduced visibility and tiredness can make night-time driving more hazardous. Defensive drivers should take extra care when driving in low-light conditions, ensuring that they are well-rested and that their headlights are functioning correctly.

Techniques for Maintaining Control

Maintaining control of your vehicle at all times is one of the cornerstones of defensive driving. In any driving situation, it's crucial to ensure that your vehicle is responsive to your commands and that you can manoeuvre it safely through any obstacles or challenges. This requires both skill and attention to detail.

Techniques for maintaining control begin with the basics, such as keeping a firm but relaxed grip on the steering wheel. It's essential to avoid gripping the wheel too tightly, as this can lead to muscle fatigue and a delayed response when quick steering adjustments are necessary. A relaxed grip ensures that you can make smooth, controlled turns and corrections when needed.

Another important technique for maintaining control is adjusting your seat and mirrors to optimize your field of vision. This helps you maintain awareness of your surroundings and react promptly to changes in traffic conditions. You should always ensure that your side mirrors and rear-view mirror are properly adjusted before starting your drive, and periodically check them while driving to stay aware of other vehicles.

Maintaining control also involves properly managing your speed and distance relative to other vehicles. Speeding can lead to reduced reaction time, especially when driving in heavy traffic or adverse conditions. By driving at a safe speed and leaving enough space between your vehicle and the one ahead, you can avoid collisions and have more time to react to sudden stops or changes in traffic.

Moreover, when cornering, make sure to slow down and steer gently. Sharp turns taken at high speeds can cause a vehicle to lose traction and spin out. If you feel the car beginning to slide, it's important to steer gently in the direction of the slide to regain control. In icy or slippery conditions, reducing speed and avoiding sudden movements is key to maintaining control.

Finally, ensure that your vehicle's tires are in good condition. Properly inflated and well-maintained tires are essential for maintaining control, especially in emergency situations. Tires with sufficient tread offer better grip on the road, reducing the risk of skidding and increasing your ability to stop or steer quickly in an emergency.

Techniques for maintaining control include:

- Proper grip on the steering wheel
- Regular mirror adjustments

- Safe speed management and following distances
- Gentle cornering and gradual steering inputs
- Ensuring tire condition and pressure are optimal

Collision Avoidance

Collision avoidance is one of the primary goals of defensive driving, and it requires proactive techniques to ensure the safety of both the driver and other road users. By anticipating potential hazards and acting pre-emptively, drivers can avoid situations that might lead to accidents.

The first technique for avoiding collisions is to always maintain a safe following distance. The general rule of thumb is the "three-second rule," which states that you should stay at least three seconds behind the vehicle in front of you. In adverse conditions such as rain or fog, it's important to increase this distance to allow for extra stopping time. The greater the distance between you and the vehicle ahead, the more time you have to react if they suddenly brake or change lanes.

Another important technique is scanning the road ahead for potential hazards. This includes keeping an eye out for vehicles that may be merging into your lane, pedestrians crossing the street, or animals that may dart across the road. By scanning far enough ahead, you can anticipate potential risks and adjust your speed or position to avoid a collision.

Avoiding distractions is also crucial for collision avoidance. Distracted driving is one of the leading causes of accidents, and it's important to focus your full attention on the road. Avoid using your phone, eating, or engaging in other activities that take your focus away from driving.

In emergency situations, it's important to act quickly but safely. If you are approaching an obstacle and cannot stop in time, swerving to avoid it might be the best option. However, swerving should be done carefully to avoid losing control of the vehicle or colliding with other objects. If you cannot avoid the obstacle entirely, it's often safer to aim for the softest area, such as a grassy shoulder, rather than hitting hard objects like guardrails or trees.

Finally, defensive drivers are always prepared for the unexpected. This means being mentally ready to react to sudden changes in traffic conditions, such as a vehicle braking unexpectedly or another driver swerving into your lane. By staying calm and focused, you can avoid panic reactions that might lead to a collision.

Emergency Manoeuvres

Emergency manoeuvres are critical skills that every defensive driver must master. These techniques help drivers react quickly and safely in situations where accidents are imminent or have already occurred. The ability to perform emergency manoeuvres with precision can prevent accidents and minimize their severity.

One of the most essential emergency manoeuvres is the emergency stop. When a driver realizes that a collision is imminent, they must be able to stop the vehicle as quickly as possible. To perform an emergency stop, apply full pressure to the brake pedal without locking the wheels. In vehicles equipped with anti-lock braking systems (ABS), it's important to apply firm, continuous pressure to the brake pedal. ABS will prevent the wheels from locking up, ensuring the driver can maintain steering control while braking.

Another important emergency manoeuvre is the evasive swerve. When a collision is imminent and stopping won't be enough to avoid an obstacle, swerving may be necessary. This manoeuvre should be executed quickly and smoothly, without jerking the steering wheel. It's important to check for other obstacles, such as other vehicles or guardrails, before swerving to ensure the manoeuvre doesn't cause a secondary collision.

In cases of hydroplaning, which occurs when the vehicle's tires lose contact with the road due to wet conditions, it's crucial to remain calm and take appropriate action. Avoid slamming on the brakes or making sharp turns, as this can cause the vehicle to spin out of control. Instead, gently ease off the accelerator and steer in the direction you want the vehicle to go. Once the tires regain traction, you can resume normal driving.

Finally, if you are involved in a collision, knowing how to respond appropriately is essential. First, ensure that you are safe and that any passengers are unharmed. If the collision is minor, you can move your vehicle out of the flow of traffic. If there are injuries or significant damage, it's important to call emergency services immediately and exchange information with the other driver. Never leave the scene of an accident, as doing so can result in serious legal consequences.

QUESTIONNAIRE

1. When driving defensively, how should a driver respond when another vehicle rapidly changes lanes into their path?

A) Speed up to regain a safer distance
B) Maintain speed and allow the vehicle to pass

C) Immediately brake hard to stop
D) Change lanes without signalling

Answer: B) Maintain speed and allow the vehicle to pass
Explanation: When another vehicle changes lanes rapidly into your path, it's essential to remain calm and avoid sudden movements. Maintaining speed and allowing the vehicle to pass ensures the driver remains in control and prevents escalation of the situation.

2. Which of the following is a primary principle of defensive driving?

A) Always drive at the maximum speed limit
B) Assume all other drivers will follow the rules
C) Constantly scan the environment for potential hazards
D) Focus only on the vehicle directly in front of you

Answer: C) Constantly scan the environment for potential hazards
Explanation: Defensive driving requires drivers to be aware of everything happening around them, not just focusing on the vehicle in front. Constant scanning helps identify hazards early, allowing time for proactive adjustments to speed, position, or even stopping if necessary.

3. What is the best action to take if you find yourself driving too fast for road conditions, such as wet or icy roads?

A) Continue driving at the current speed until the conditions improve
B) Increase speed to clear wet spots faster
C) Reduce speed immediately to maintain control and increase stopping distance

D) Keep a steady speed without changing until you reach a safer area

Answer: C) Reduce speed immediately to maintain control and increase stopping distance
Explanation: Reducing speed in adverse conditions such as wet or icy roads increases the driver's control over the vehicle and gives more time to react. Slowing down also provides additional distance for stopping.

4. In a situation where a driver feels the vehicle is hydroplaning, what is the correct response?

A) Slam the brakes to stop as quickly as possible
B) Steer sharply to regain control
C) Gradually reduce speed by easing off the accelerator and gently steering
D) Increase speed to get through the water patch faster

Answer: C) Gradually reduce speed by easing off the accelerator and gently steering
Explanation: During hydroplaning, the tires lose contact with the road surface. Gradually easing off the accelerator and steering gently helps restore contact between the tires and road, avoiding a spin-out.

5. How can a driver best avoid a collision when another driver makes an unexpected lane change directly in front of them?

A) Attempt to overtake the vehicle from the other side
B) Honk the horn and flash lights to warn the driver
C) Maintain a safe following distance, slow down, and be ready to stop if necessary

D) Speed up to pass the vehicle and reduce the risk of being rear-ended

Answer: C) Maintain a safe following distance, slow down, and be ready to stop if necessary
Explanation: Maintaining a safe distance, slowing down, and being ready to stop is the safest response. This provides space and time to avoid a potential collision if the driver in front makes an abrupt stop or further lane changes.

6. What is the primary reason for maintaining a safe following distance when driving?

A) To prevent other drivers from tailgating
B) To allow ample time for reacting to sudden stops or changes in traffic
C) To be able to navigate around slower vehicles
D) To prevent getting stuck behind larger vehicles like trucks

Answer: B) To allow ample time for reacting to sudden stops or changes in traffic
Explanation: A safe following distance is crucial for providing the time needed to react to any unexpected changes in the road conditions or actions of other drivers. It also allows the driver enough space to stop or manoeuvre if necessary.

7. Which of the following should a driver do when navigating a construction zone?

A) Speed up to quickly pass through the area
B) Follow the speed limit as it may not be enforced in construction zones
C) Remain alert, reduce speed, and follow posted signs for

construction zones

D) Change lanes frequently to avoid delays

Answer: C) Remain alert, reduce speed, and follow posted signs for construction zones

Explanation: Construction zones are high-risk areas due to workers and equipment in the area. Drivers must reduce speed, remain aware of changing conditions, and adhere to posted signage, as the rules in these areas often differ from regular driving conditions.

8. In which situation is it most important to adjust your driving speed to account for defensive driving principles?

A) When driving on a straight, clear highway

B) When driving in congested city traffic

C) When driving through a small town with no traffic signals

D) When driving on a well-lit road at night

Answer: B) When driving in congested city traffic

Explanation: Congested city traffic presents numerous risks due to frequent stops, unexpected lane changes, and pedestrians. Defensive drivers must reduce their speed, increase following distance, and remain vigilant to avoid accidents in such environments.

9. How should a defensive driver react to a vehicle that is tailgating them?

A) Speed up to get away from the tailgater

B) Slam the brakes to teach them a lesson

C) Change lanes safely to allow the tailgater to pass

D) Ignore the tailgater and continue driving at the same speed

Answer: C) Change lanes safely to allow the tailgater to pass
Explanation: The safest way to deal with a tailgater is to allow them to pass. Continuing to drive at the same speed or attempting to brake suddenly can escalate the situation. By changing lanes safely, you avoid unnecessary tension and maintain control.

10. Which of the following is an essential aspect of maintaining control of your vehicle during adverse weather conditions?

A) Driving faster to reduce the time spent in hazardous conditions
B) Using your vehicle's cruise control to maintain a steady speed
C) Keeping both hands on the wheel and slowing down
D) Ignoring the weather and focusing solely on the road signs

Answer: C) Keeping both hands on the wheel and slowing down
Explanation: Maintaining both hands on the wheel allows for better control of the vehicle, particularly in slippery or windy conditions. Slowing down is essential for increasing stopping distance and reaction time, reducing the risk of losing control.

Chapter 7

Utah Laws 2024

Utah, like every state in the United States, has developed a comprehensive set of traffic laws aimed at ensuring safety on its roads, enhancing the driving experience, and protecting both drivers and pedestrians. The state's traffic laws evolve annually, adapting to changes in road conditions, technological advancements, and societal needs. For 2024, Utah's laws reflect an ongoing effort to balance the interests of public safety with practical driving considerations.

One of the most notable aspects of Utah's laws is the state's strong focus on DUI (Driving Under the Influence) regulations. Utah's stringent stance on impaired driving is among the most aggressive in the nation, with legal blood alcohol concentration (BAC) limits set lower than many other states. The state's emphasis on public safety is also reflected in its seatbelt and child restraint laws, which mandate the use of seat belts for all passengers, while also imposing strict guidelines on child safety seats.

Additionally, Utah's approach to distracted driving has garnered attention, with laws that specifically target the use of mobile devices while driving. These regulations are designed to reduce accidents caused by texting, phone calls, or any other distractions that divert the driver's attention away from the road. Other areas of concern include regulations around beach driving, the process of reporting accidents, and insurance requirements for drivers. The state's rules for beach driving are designed to ensure that recreational driving on beaches does not interfere with environmental preservation or public safety. Similarly, Utah requires drivers to carry a minimum level of auto insurance to protect themselves and others in the event of an accident.

The year 2024 also sees a greater emphasis on the use of modern technologies for reporting accidents and filing claims. With the increasing prevalence of smartphone apps, Utah has made efforts to streamline the process of filing accident reports and insurance claims, making it easier for drivers to comply with state laws and for insurance companies to process claims efficiently.

DUI and DWI Regulations

Utah's laws regarding Driving Under the Influence (DUI) and Driving While Intoxicated (DWI) are among the most stringent in the United States. The state has taken a strong stance against impaired driving, prioritizing road safety above all else.

The legal blood alcohol concentration (BAC) limit in Utah is 0.05%, which is lower than the standard 0.08% that applies in most other states. This means that drivers in Utah can be arrested for DUI even if their BAC is below the commonly accepted threshold. Utah's approach is founded on the principle that any level of alcohol or drug impairment can significantly affect a driver's ability to operate a vehicle safely.

DUI offenses are classified into different categories based on the driver's BAC and whether any aggravating factors are involved, such as prior DUI convictions or the presence of minors in the vehicle. A first-time offense typically results in fines, mandatory alcohol education classes, and a license suspension. Subsequent offenses lead to harsher penalties, including longer license suspensions, higher fines, mandatory jail time, and the installation of an ignition interlock device.

Driving While Intoxicated (DWI) laws in Utah also target drivers who are under the influence of drugs, including marijuana, prescription medications, or any other substance that impairs a person's ability to drive. A DWI charge can result in similar penalties to a DUI charge, with the added complexity of prosecuting impaired drivers who may not have alcohol in their system.

For those arrested for DUI or DWI, refusing to take a chemical test can lead to an automatic license suspension and may serve as evidence of impairment in court. Law enforcement in Utah has the right to use roadside sobriety tests and chemical testing to determine a driver's impairment level.

Seat Belt and Child Restraint Laws

In Utah, the laws governing seat belt use and child restraints are clear and strictly enforced, with the aim of reducing the risk of injury and fatality in traffic accidents. The seat belt law applies to all drivers and passengers, regardless of age, and requires that seat belts be worn at all times when the vehicle is in motion.

For adults, the law mandates that both the driver and all passengers must be properly restrained in the vehicle. If any passenger is found not wearing a seat belt, the driver can be fined for the violation. The law also extends to rear-seat passengers, and those over the age of 16 must also be wearing a seatbelt.

For children, Utah has specific requirements for child restraint systems based on the child's age, weight, and height. Children under the age of 8 must be secured in a child safety seat or booster seat appropriate for their size. This includes rear-facing seats for infants, forward-facing seats for toddlers, and booster seats for older children who have outgrown their car seats but are still too small for regular seat belts.

Once a child reaches the age of 8 or a height of 57 inches, they are no longer required to use a booster seat, but they must still wear a seatbelt. The law also mandates that children under the age of 16 must be properly secured in the vehicle, whether in a seat belt or child restraint.

Distracted Driving Laws and Mobile Device Laws

Utah has implemented strict laws regarding distracted driving, aiming to minimize the risk of accidents caused by drivers who are not paying attention to the road. One of the main contributors to distracted driving is the use of mobile devices, which is regulated under Utah's mobile device laws.

The law prohibits drivers from using a hand-held mobile phone to text, browse the internet, or use any other application while driving. This includes the use of social media, taking photos, or sending emails. The primary concern is that these activities take a driver's attention away from the road, which increases the likelihood of accidents.

Utah's law allows drivers to use hands-free devices for making calls, but texting or emailing while driving is explicitly prohibited, even when the vehicle is stopped at a traffic light. Drivers who violate the mobile device law can face fines, and subsequent offenses can result in increased penalties.

The state also prohibits all drivers, regardless of age, from using mobile devices for any purpose while driving in school zones, highway work zones, or construction zones, where distractions are especially dangerous.

The enforcement of these laws is primarily conducted by police officers who observe drivers using their mobile devices while operating a vehicle. Officers may also use technology to monitor and identify distracted drivers during routine traffic stops.

Beach Driving Regulations

While beach driving is not common across the state of Utah, there are areas where driving on beaches is allowed, particularly in areas near the Great Salt Lake and other designated recreational areas. However, beach driving is subject to specific rules and regulations to ensure safety and protect the environment.

Drivers must stay within the designated areas where beach driving is permitted. These areas are typically marked with signs, and failure to comply with these markers can result in fines. Drivers must also exercise extreme caution when driving on beaches, as the soft sand can make it easy to become stuck. It's essential for drivers to be aware of tidal changes, as water levels can fluctuate and create hazardous conditions on the sand.

The use of all-terrain vehicles (ATVs) and off-road vehicles is regulated, and drivers must ensure their vehicles are equipped for the conditions. Additionally, driving on beaches that are environmentally sensitive, such as those with nesting birds or fragile ecosystems, is strictly prohibited. Environmental considerations are a priority, and drivers must be careful to avoid damaging the natural habitat.

Beach driving requires a permit in many areas, and it is advisable for drivers to check with local authorities before embarking on such activities. Finally, the general speed limits on beaches are reduced to prevent accidents, especially around pedestrians and wildlife.

Reporting Accidents in Utah

In Utah, the process of reporting accidents is governed by strict regulations designed to ensure that all parties involved in an accident are properly documented, and that the incident is investigated thoroughly by the appropriate authorities. Accidents involving injuries, fatalities, or property damage above a certain threshold must be reported to law enforcement.

When to Report an Accident

Under Utah law, you are required to report an accident when it results in any of the following:

1. **Injury or Death**: If anyone is injured or killed in the accident, it must be reported to law enforcement immediately. This is critical for ensuring that proper medical care is provided to those involved, and that a legal record is established.

2. **Property Damage**: If the property damage in an accident exceeds $1,500, it must be reported. This includes damage to vehicles, structures, or public property. If the property damage is under this threshold, reporting may not be required unless the accident involves an injury or death.

3. **Hit-and-Run Accidents**: If one of the parties involved in the accident leaves the scene without exchanging information, the incident must be reported to law enforcement

immediately. Leaving the scene of an accident is illegal and can lead to criminal charges.

4. **Accidents Involving a Government Vehicle**: Accidents that involve a government-owned vehicle must always be reported, regardless of whether there is injury or significant damage.

How to Report an Accident

If you are involved in an accident that requires reporting, follow these steps:

1. **Ensure Safety**: First and foremost, ensure your safety and the safety of others involved in the accident. If anyone is injured, call 911 immediately for medical assistance. If possible, move vehicles to the side of the road to prevent further accidents.

2. **Contact Law Enforcement**: After ensuring safety, call local law enforcement to report the accident. Depending on the location, you may need to contact city police, county sheriffs, or state troopers. Be prepared to provide your location, details of the accident, and the number of people involved.

3. **Provide Accurate Information**: When law enforcement arrives, provide an accurate account of what happened. This includes details about the time of the accident, weather conditions, any contributing factors, and any personal injuries. Failing to provide accurate information can result in legal consequences.

4. **Complete an Accident Report**: In many cases, law enforcement will complete an official accident report at the

scene. You may also be required to fill out an accident report form, especially if law enforcement is not able to attend immediately. This can often be done online or through the Department of Public Safety.

5. **Exchange Information**: While law enforcement handles the investigation, you should exchange information with the other drivers involved in the accident. This includes names, addresses, phone numbers, driver's license numbers, and insurance information. If possible, take note of the vehicle's license plate number, make, model, and color.

6. **File a Report with the Department of Public Safety**: If law enforcement does not respond to the scene or if you need to file a report after the fact, you must submit an accident report to the Utah Department of Public Safety (DPS) within 10 days of the accident. This can be done online, and there may be penalties if the report is not filed within the required timeframe.

7. **Follow-Up with Your Insurance Company**: Once the accident is reported to law enforcement and you've exchanged information, you should also contact your insurance provider. Be sure to provide them with all necessary documentation, including the accident report, photographs, and witness statements if available.

8. **Medical Records and Claims**: If injuries were sustained during the accident, be sure to keep track of any medical treatments or bills, as these will be important when processing insurance claims.

Legal Consequences for Failing to Report

Failing to report an accident when required can lead to legal consequences, including fines and possible criminal charges. If a hit-and-run accident occurs, leaving the scene can result in severe penalties, including suspension of your driver's license, hefty fines, and potential jail time.

It is critical that all accidents meeting the criteria are reported accurately and in a timely manner. Failure to comply with reporting requirements could impact your ability to file an insurance claim or pursue legal action in the future.

Insurance Requirements/Information

In Utah, drivers are required to carry a minimum level of insurance coverage to operate a motor vehicle legally. The purpose of these requirements is to protect all parties involved in accidents and ensure that drivers can cover the costs of injuries and damages resulting from their actions. The state's auto insurance laws set minimum coverage limits, and drivers are encouraged to carry additional coverage for extra protection.

Minimum Insurance Requirements in Utah

As of 2024, Utah law requires drivers to carry the following minimum insurance coverage:

1. **Bodily Injury Liability**: This covers medical expenses for injuries that other people sustain in an accident for which you are at fault. The minimum required coverage is $25,000 per person and $65,000 per accident.

2. **Property Damage Liability**: This coverage pays for damage to another person's property (e.g., vehicles, fences,

or buildings) caused by your actions. The minimum required coverage is $15,000.

3. **Personal Injury Protection (PIP)**: Utah is a no-fault state for auto insurance, meaning that each driver's own insurance pays for their medical costs regardless of who was at fault in the accident. The minimum PIP coverage required is $3,000.

Additional Coverage Options

While the state's minimum insurance requirements provide basic coverage, drivers are strongly encouraged to carry additional coverage for better protection:

1. **Collision Coverage**: This pays for damage to your own vehicle resulting from a collision, regardless of fault. It typically comes with a deductible that you must pay out-of-pocket before the insurance company pays the remainder of the claim.

2. **Comprehensive Coverage**: This type of coverage protects against damage to your vehicle that is not caused by a collision, such as damage from weather events, theft, or vandalism.

3. **Uninsured/Underinsured Motorist Coverage**: This protects you in the event of an accident with a driver who either has no insurance or insufficient insurance to cover the damages. Although not required by law, it is highly recommended.

4. **Rental Car Coverage**: If your vehicle is damaged and needs repairs, this optional coverage helps pay for the cost of a rental car while your car is being fixed.

Insurance Information and Claims Process

When purchasing insurance in Utah, it's essential to understand the terms of your policy. Each policy will include details about the coverage limits, deductibles, and the circumstances under which you can file a claim. Insurance companies may offer different levels of coverage and discounts, so it's important to shop around for the best option for your needs.

In the event of an accident, filing an insurance claim typically involves the following steps:

1. **Contact Your Insurance Company**: Report the accident to your insurance provider as soon as possible, providing all relevant details, such as the accident report, witness statements, and medical information if applicable.

2. **Assessment of Damages**: The insurance company will assign an adjuster to assess the damages and determine the cost of repairs or medical bills. They may ask for photographs, repair estimates, or additional documentation.

3. **Claim Approval and Payment**: Once the adjuster reviews the claim, the insurance company will approve or deny it based on the terms of your policy. If the claim is approved, they will provide payment to cover damages or medical expenses up to your coverage limits, minus your deductible.

4. **Dispute Resolution**: If you disagree with the insurance company's decision regarding coverage or the payout amount, you have the right to dispute the decision. This can often be done through mediation or arbitration, depending on your policy's terms.

Understanding the ins and outs of auto insurance is critical for drivers in Utah to ensure they comply with state requirements and protect themselves in the event of an accident. Be sure to review your policy regularly and update it as necessary to keep your coverage aligned with your needs.

Chapter 8

After the Test: Next Steps

Congratulations! You have successfully completed the steps to pass your driving exam in Utah, marking a significant milestone in your journey to becoming a responsible and skilled driver. This accomplishment reflects not only your knowledge of traffic laws and road safety but also your commitment to being an active, aware, and law-abiding member of the driving community. Now that you have passed the exam, it's time to move forward with the next steps toward obtaining your driver's license and ensuring that your driving experience is safe, efficient, and legally compliant.

The next steps are crucial as they involve finalizing the legal aspects of driving, such as vehicle registration, insurance requirements, and understanding the rules and responsibilities that come with holding a driver's license. It's also essential to focus on maintaining a clean driving record, understanding the consequences of violations, and taking proactive steps to ensure your continued success on the road.

In this section, we will discuss how to register and renew your vehicle, how to maintain a clean driving record, and what to do after obtaining your driver's license. You will also be introduced to the responsibility that comes with holding a license, including rules surrounding traffic violations and their impact on your privileges. With this comprehensive knowledge, you will be prepared for a lifetime of safe driving and full compliance with Utah's traffic laws.

Vehicle Registration and Renewal

Vehicle registration and renewal are essential components of legally operating a vehicle in Utah. The process is designed to ensure that vehicles meet the state's safety standards and comply with environmental regulations. Vehicle registration serves as proof that the vehicle is properly documented and insured to be on the road.

The vehicle registration process in Utah begins when you purchase a vehicle or move to Utah. All vehicles that are driven on public roads must be registered with the Utah Division of Motor Vehicles (DMV). To register a vehicle, the first step is to gather necessary documents. These include the vehicle title, proof of identification, proof of insurance, and an emissions inspection certificate if required. New residents or individuals who have just purchased a vehicle will also need to bring proof of residency, such as a utility bill or lease agreement.

The first step to registration involves completing an application form provided by the DMV, either online or in person. The DMV will assess your vehicle for compliance with the registration requirements, including safety and environmental checks. Once all requirements are met, you will be issued a license plate, a registration sticker, and a certificate of registration. The registration sticker is placed on your vehicle's license plate and must be renewed every year to ensure your vehicle remains legally operational.

Renewing your vehicle registration is a straightforward process that takes place every 12 months. The Utah DMV typically sends out a renewal notice a few weeks before the expiration date of your registration. This notice will contain all the information you need to renew your registration, including the amount due and any required emissions or safety inspections. You can renew your registration online, by mail, or in person at a DMV office. If you choose to renew online, you'll need to have your vehicle identification number (VIN) and license plate number available.

In addition to the basic renewal process, there are specific situations where your vehicle may require additional actions for registration. For example, if you have moved to a new address or made modifications to your vehicle, you must update the DMV records. If you have failed to renew your registration in a timely manner, you may face late fees or penalties. In extreme cases, driving a vehicle with expired registration may result in fines, impoundment of the vehicle, or suspension of driving privileges.

It is important to note that the renewal process also requires proof of valid insurance coverage, so it's essential to maintain continuous insurance on your vehicle. If your insurance policy lapses or is cancelled, you will not be able to renew your registration until you have obtained valid insurance.

For individuals who own multiple vehicles, the Utah DMV provides an option to renew vehicle registrations in bulk. Additionally, there are specialized registration options available for certain vehicle types, such as commercial vehicles, trailers, and motorcycles, which may have different fees or requirements.

In addition to standard registration, you can opt to participate in Utah's emissions testing program, which requires certain vehicles to undergo testing to ensure they meet environmental standards. Some counties in Utah may also have additional requirements for registration and emissions testing, so it's essential to check with your local DMV office for specific guidelines.

Vehicle registration renewal is also an opportunity to ensure that your vehicle is properly maintained and compliant with road safety standards. Regular inspections, including those for emissions and safety, should be a part of your vehicle's care routine. Keeping track of your registration expiration date, paying the fees on time, and ensuring that your vehicle is in good condition will help you avoid unnecessary fines and legal trouble.

Maintaining a Clean Driving Record

Maintaining a clean driving record is essential for ensuring a long, successful driving career and for avoiding unnecessary penalties. A clean driving record reflects your commitment to safety, responsibility, and compliance with traffic laws. It is important to understand how traffic violations, accidents, and other infractions can affect your record, insurance premiums, and even your driving privileges.

A clean driving record is crucial because it directly impacts your ability to maintain affordable car insurance. Drivers with violations or accidents on their record may face higher premiums, as they are perceived as higher-risk drivers by insurance companies. Moreover, a history of violations or accidents can lead to suspension or revocation of your driver's license, depending on the severity of the infraction.

To maintain a clean driving record, it is essential to follow traffic laws and drive responsibly at all times. Avoid speeding, running red lights, and engaging in reckless driving behaviour. Always use seat belts, maintain a safe following distance, and be mindful of road signs and signals. Staying sober and avoiding distractions while driving are also crucial to preventing violations and accidents.

Driving defensively is one of the most effective ways to avoid accidents and prevent violations. Stay alert, be prepared for unexpected changes in traffic conditions, and always give yourself enough time to react to potential hazards. Avoid aggressive driving, such as tailgating or weaving in and out of traffic, which can increase the likelihood of accidents.

To further safeguard your driving record, consider taking a defensive driving course. Many states, including Utah, offer courses that can help improve driving skills and reduce the likelihood of accidents. Completing these courses may also result in the reduction of points on your driving record, which could help lower insurance premiums and prevent license suspension.

Regularly checking your driving record is also a good practice. If any mistakes or discrepancies are found, address them promptly with the appropriate authorities. Correcting errors on your record can prevent unnecessary penalties or issues when renewing your license or insurance.

Tips for Keeping a Clean Driving Record

- **Obey Traffic Laws**: Always follow speed limits, traffic signals, and road signs to avoid citations.

- **Avoid Distractions**: Keep your attention on the road and avoid using mobile devices while driving.

- **Drive Defensively**: Stay alert, anticipate potential hazards, and maintain safe distances from other vehicles.

- **Take Defensive Driving Courses**: Participate in driver improvement courses to enhance your skills and reduce violations.

- **Be Courteous**: Practice patience and avoid aggressive driving behaviours, such as tailgating or road rage.

- **Inspect Your Vehicle**: Ensure your car is properly maintained and safe to drive to prevent mechanical failures and accidents.

- **Stay Sober**: Never drive under the influence of alcohol or drugs.

- **Monitor Your Record**: Regularly check your driving record to ensure there are no errors or discrepancies.

APPENDIX

Glossary of Terms

In order to understand the driving laws, practices, and regulations more effectively, it is essential to be familiar with the following terms commonly used throughout this handbook:

ABCs of Defensive Driving: Refers to the fundamental principles and techniques for safe driving, emphasizing awareness, caution, and preparedness to avoid accidents.

Admission of Guilt: A statement made by a driver acknowledging a traffic violation, often used as a means to settle a ticket without going to court.

Alcohol Concentration (AC): The percentage of alcohol in a driver's bloodstream, commonly used to measure intoxication. In Utah, a BAC (Blood Alcohol Concentration) of 0.08% or higher is considered impaired.

Blind Spot: Areas around a vehicle that are not visible to the driver, typically due to obstructions in the mirrors or vehicle structure. Drivers must check their blind spots before changing lanes or merging.

Commercial Driver's License (CDL): A license required to operate large or heavy vehicles, including buses, trucks, and vehicles that carry hazardous materials.

Defensive Driving: A set of driving strategies aimed at anticipating potential hazards on the road and taking proactive steps to avoid them.

DUI (Driving Under the Influence): Refers to operating a motor vehicle while impaired by alcohol, drugs, or any other substance that affects driving ability.

DWI (Driving While Intoxicated): Similar to DUI, this term specifically refers to driving while impaired by alcohol or drugs. In some states, the terms DUI and DWI are used interchangeably.

Emissions Inspection: A state-required process to check that a vehicle's emissions system is functioning properly and that the vehicle meets environmental standards.

Field Sobriety Test (FST): A series of physical and mental exercises used by law enforcement to assess whether a driver is under the influence of alcohol or drugs.

Insurance Liability: A form of insurance coverage that compensates others for injury or damage caused by the policyholder while driving.

Intersection: The point at which two or more roads meet or cross. Proper navigation of intersections is essential for road safety.

License Suspension: The temporary revocation of a driver's license as a penalty for certain traffic violations, including driving under the influence or accumulating too many points on the driving record.

Point System: A system in which points are added to a driver's record for traffic violations. Accumulating too many points can lead to license suspension.

Primary Collision Factor (PCF): The cause or reason that contributes most directly to a traffic accident, such as speeding, running a red light, or driving while impaired.

Traffic Citation: A notice issued by law enforcement to a driver for violating traffic laws, such as speeding, illegal parking, or failure to stop at a stop sign.

Vehicle Registration: The process of registering a vehicle with the DMV to legally operate it on public roads. This process involves proving ownership, meeting safety standards, and maintaining insurance coverage.

Yield: The act of giving way to other drivers or pedestrians to ensure safety when navigating intersections or merging into traffic.

Utah DMV Contact Information

For any questions regarding driver's licenses, vehicle registration, driving records, or other motor vehicle services, you can contact the Utah Department of Motor Vehicles (DMV) through the following channels:

Utah Department of Motor Vehicles
Website: https://dmv.utah.gov
Phone Number: 1-800-DMV-UTAH (1-800-368-8824)
Office Hours: Monday to Friday, 8:00 AM to 5:00 PM
Location:
Utah DMV Main Office
4501 South 2700 West
Salt Lake City, UT 84114

For vehicle registration, driver's license applications, and other DMV-related services, it's recommended to visit the DMV website for updates, office locations, and available online services. Many DMV services are accessible through the online portal, including scheduling appointments, paying fees, and renewing licenses and vehicle registrations.

Additional Resources for Drivers

Here are additional resources for drivers that provide valuable information, support, and services related to safe driving, vehicle maintenance, insurance, and more:

1. **Utah Highway Safety Office**
   Website: https://highwaysafety.utah.gov
   The Utah Highway Safety Office offers tips on safe driving, accident prevention, and impaired driving awareness.

2. **Utah Department of Public Safety**
   Website: https://dps.utah.gov
   Provides information on public safety initiatives, including traffic laws, emergency response services, and disaster preparedness.

3. **National Highway Traffic Safety Administration (NHTSA)**
   Website: https://www.nhtsa.gov
   The NHTSA offers national guidelines for road safety, information on vehicle recalls, and education on driving under the influence (DUI).

4. **American Automobile Association (AAA)**
   Website: https://www.aaa.com
   AAA provides various resources, including maps, driving

safety tips, insurance information, and emergency roadside assistance services.

5. **Utah Drivers Education**
   Website: https://driversed.com
   A resource for individuals seeking to complete drivers education courses, offering online courses and in-person classes.

6. **Utah Insurance Department**
   Website: https://insurance.utah.gov
   The Utah Insurance Department provides resources for understanding insurance requirements, filing complaints, and learning about policy details.

7. **Insurance Information Institute (III)**
   Website: https://www.iii.org
   Offers educational materials on all types of insurance, including automobile, and provides statistics and reports related to vehicle insurance.

8. **Utah State Tax Commission**
   Website: https://tax.utah.gov
   Provides details on the state's vehicle registration, title transfer processes, and sales tax for vehicle purchases.

9. **Centers for Disease Control and Prevention (CDC) – Motor Vehicle Safety**
   Website: https://www.cdc.gov/motorvehiclesafety
   The CDC offers extensive information on preventing car crashes, including tips on seatbelt use, child safety, and distracted driving prevention.

10. **National Safety Council (NSC)**
    Website: https://www.nsc.org
    Provides resources for safe driving, accident prevention,
    and information on traffic safety legislation and programs.

These resources are designed to help drivers maintain safe driving practices, navigate Utah's driving regulations, and stay informed about changes in laws and safety standards. It is important to regularly check these websites and remain proactive about your responsibilities as a driver.

29677396R00086